Learning C# by Developing Games with Unity 3D Beginner's Guide

Learn the fundamentals of C# to create scripts for your GameObjects

Terry Norton

PUBLISHING

BIRMINGHAM - MUMBAI

About the Author

Terry Norton was born and raised in California. During the Vietnam era, he served six and half years in the US Air Force. While in the military, he was trained in electronics for electronic counter-measures. Upon discharge, he earned his Electrical Engineering degree, and later working for Joslyn Defense Systems in Vermont, designing and developing test equipment for the US Navy.

When personal computers came on the scene, he took an interest in building computers, but never quite delved deep into the programming side. It wasn't until 2004 that programming peaked his interest. He began writing articles for OS/2 Magazine to teach C++ programming. Unfortunately, damaging his left hand in a snowblower accident in 2005 ended his writing for a couple years.

IBM abandoned OS/2, so Terry bought his first Apple computer in early 2006. He tried a few times to learn Objective-C, but work and family always seemed to sidetrack his efforts. It wasn't until about 2010 when he discovered Unity and the need to write scripts, that he finally made some progress into the programming world. He began writing an online tutorial for UnityScript titled *UnityScript for Noobs*. It was a basic tutorial for beginners made available just before Unite 2011.

Since then, Terry has been learning C# for writing scripts for Unity. Packt Publishing noticed *UnityScript for Noobs* and asked if he would be interested in writing a book about learning UnityScript. He declined. He felt that C# was a better language, and his heart just wasn't into UnityScript any longer. Two weeks later, Packt offered him the opportunity to write a book about learning C# for Unity. He jumped on it.

I want to thank my daughter Emily Norton, the artist in the family, for helping me with the graphic's design.

About the Reviewers

Gaurav Garg was born in Delhi. He is a Computer Applications graduate from Indira Gandhi University and has passed his higher secondary from the CBSE Board. During his under-graduate studies, he started his career as an indie game programmer, but didn't gain success because of a lack of or say, no experience. After this, he learnt that passion is not the only thing for geting success; experience matters a lot. Then he joined Isis Design Service as a game programmer, where he published a few iOS titles and one web-based game. He worked there for a year and a half. Then, he moved to Jump Games, Pune, and worked on a few good game titles such as Realsteal and Dancing with the Stars. Now, he works for Mr Manvender Shukul in Lakshya Digital Pvt ltd. and has been there since the past year.

He hasn't reviewed a book before, but one of his articles was published in Game Coder Magazine. The article was on Unity3D. You can download the article from his personal website, http://gauravgarg.com/.

I would like to thanks my parents who taught me the value of hard work and an education.

I need to thanks my friends, particularly Manjith and Vibhash, who always took the time to listen, even when I was just complaining. They always are my best supporters and advisors.

Finally, I would like to thank Harshit who gives me this opportunity.

Kristian Hedeholm studied Computer Science at Aarhus University and now works as a game programmer at Serious Games Interactive in Copenhagen, Denmark. Since Kristian joined the game industry back in 2009, he has worked on a couple of released casual games. In addition to this, he is also the chairman of an association called Young Game Developers, which aims to spread information about game development among children and teenagers. In the future, Kristian will use his "computer mind" to develop artificial intelligence and dynamic difficulty adjustment systems for computer games.

When Kristian isn't developing games, teaching others to develop games, or playing games himself, he thinks about them a lot!

www.PacktPub.com

Support files, eBooks, discount offers and more

You might want to visit www.PacktPub.com for support files and downloads related to your book.

Did you know that Packt offers eBook versions of every book published, with PDF and ePub files available? You can upgrade to the eBook version at www.PacktPub.com and as a print book customer, you are entitled to a discount on the eBook copy. Get in touch with us at service@packtpub.com for more details.

At www.PacktPub.com, you can also read a collection of free technical articles, sign up for a range of free newsletters and receive exclusive discounts and offers on Packt books and eBooks.

http://PacktLib.PacktPub.com

Do you need instant solutions to your IT questions? PacktLib is Packt's online digital book library. Here, you can access, read and search across Packt's entire library of books.

Why Subscribe?

- Fully searchable across every book published by Packt
- Copy and paste, print and bookmark content
- On demand and accessible via web browser

Free Access for Packt account holders

If you have an account with Packt at www.PacktPub.com, you can use this to access PacktLib today and view nine entirely free books. Simply use your login credentials for immediate access.

Table of Contents

Preface

Unity has become one of the most popular game engines for developers, from the amateur hobbyist to the professional working in a large studio. Unity used to be considered a 3D tool, but with the release of Unity 4.3, it now has dedicated 2D tools. This will expand Unity's use even more.

Developers love its object-oriented drag-and-drop user interface which makes creating a game or interactive product so easy. Despite the visual ease of working in Unity, there is a need to understand some basic programming to be able to write scripts for GameObjects. For game developers that have any programming knowledge, learning how to write scripts is quite easy. For the the artist coming to Unity, creating the visual aspects of a game is a breeze, but writing scripts may appear to be a giant roadblock.

This book is for those with no concept of programming. I introduce the building blocks, that is, basic concepts of programming using everyday examples you are familiar with. Also, my approach to teaching is not what you will find in the typical programming book. In the end, you will learn the basics of C#, but I will spoon-feed you the details as they are needed.

I will take you through the steps needed to create a simple game, with the focus not being the game itself but on how the many separate sections of code come together to make a working game. I will also introduce the concept of a State Machine to organize code into simple, game controlling blocks. At the end, you will be saying "Wow! I can't believe how easy that was!"

What this book covers

Chapter 1, Discovering Your Hidden Scripting Skills, explains that the very first thing you need to do is overcome your perceived fear of writing scripts. You'll see that writing scripts is very similar to many of your daily routines. We also have a first look at Unity's scripting documentation. Finally, we see how to create a C# script file in Unity.

Chapter 2, Introducing the Building Blocks for Unity Scripts, explains that there are two primary building blocks for writing code, variables and methods. This chapter introduces the concepts of a variable and a method. With these two building blocks, we look into the concept of a "class," a container of variables and methods used to create Unity Components. Finally, communication between GameObjects is discussed by introducing Dot Syntax.

Chapter 3, Getting into the Details of Variables, explains using variables in detail. We see how they're used for storing data, and how the magic works to turn variables into Component properties which appear in the Unity Inspector panel.

Chapter 4, Getting into the Details of Methods, explains how methods perform the actions that take place on GameObjects. We see how to create and use methods in detail. We also look into two of Unity's most often used methods, the Start() method and the Update() method.

Chapter 5, Making Decisions in Code, explains that during gameplay, decisions have to be made about many things, just like you do in your daily life. We look at many of the ways choices are made and some of the common reasons for which decisions are required.

Chapter 6, Using Dot Syntax for Object Communication, shows us what Dot Syntax actually is, a simple address format to retrieve information or send information to other Components.

Chapter 7, Creating the Gameplay is Just a Part of the Game, shows that developing the gameplay is fun, but there are other parts needed to make a fully functional game. We look into some of the possible parts needed and how to organize all the parts by introducing the use of a State Machine.

Chapter 8, Developing the State Machine, creates a simple State Machine to show how it works, and see the simplicity it brings for controlling a game. We show how to change Scenes for a multi-level game and how to deal with GameObjects when changing to another scene.

Chapter 9, Start Building a Game and Get the Basic Structure Running, teaches us how to access and use Unity's Scripting Reference and the Reference Manual for the features we want. Then we begin creating a multi-level game using the state machine and three scenes. A Player GameObject is added and we learn how to control it.

Chapter 10, Moving Around, Collisions, and Keeping Score, shows how to move the Player around using Unity's physics system, and have cameras follow the Player's movements. We develop a GUI scoring system, start shooting projectiles at enemy objects, and see how to win or lose the game. Ultimately, we see how all the separate pieces of code come together and work together.

Chapter 11, Summarizing Your New Coding Skills, reviews the main points you learned about programming with C# and working with objects. I tell you about some of the C# and Unity features you may want to learn now that you understand the basics of C#. I will highlight the benefits of incorporating a state machine into your Unity projects. Finally, I present my favorite sources for further learning.

Appendix A, Initial State machine files, shows the initial code for the classes needed for changing States in our game. These State Machine classes are the starting point for organizing and adding game code.

Appendix B, Completed code files for Chapters 9 and 10, shows all the class and script files used for playing our completed game.

What you need for this book

You need the free version of Unity located at `http://unity3d.com/unity/download/`. The MonoDevelop code editor is included in the Unity installation.

Your computer will need to meet the minimum requirements for Unity as specified at `http://unity3d.com/unity/system-requirements.html`.

Windows: XP SP2 or later; Mac OS X "Snow Leopard" 10.6 or later. Note that Unity was not tested on server versions of Windows and OS X.

Graphics card with DirectX 9 level (shader model 2.0) capabilities. Any card made since 2004 should work.

Who this book is for

If you don't know anything about programming in general, writing code, writing scripts, or have no idea where to even begin, then this book is perfect for you. If you want to make games and need to learn how to write C# scripts or code, then this book is ideal for you.

Conventions

In this book, you will find several headings appearing frequently.

To give clear instructions of how to complete a procedure or task, we use:

Time for action – heading

1. Action 1
2. Action 2
3. Action 3

Instructions often need some extra explanation so that they make sense, so they are followed with:

What just happened?

This heading explains the working of tasks or instructions that you have just completed.

You will also find some other learning aids in the book, including:

Pop quiz – heading

These are short multiple-choice questions intended to help you test your own understanding.

Have a go hero – heading

These practical challenges give you ideas for experimenting with what you have learned.

You will also find a number of styles of text that distinguish between different kinds of information. Here are some examples of these styles, and an explanation of their meaning.

Code words in text, database table names, folder names, filenames, file extensions, pathnames, dummy URLs, user input, and Twitter handles are shown as follows: "We can include other contexts through the use of the include directive."

A block of code is set as follows:

```
public BeginState (StateManager managerRef)
{
manager = managerRef;
if(Application.loadedLevelName != "Scene0")
Application.LoadLevel("Scene0");
}
```

When we wish to draw your attention to a particular part of a code block, the relevant lines or items are set in bold:

```
if(instanceRef == null)
{
instanceRef = this;
DontDestroyOnLoad(gameObject);
}
```

Any command-line input or output is written as follows:

```
# cp /usr/src/asterisk-addons/configs/cdr_mysql.conf.sample
    /etc/asterisk/cdr_mysql.conf
```

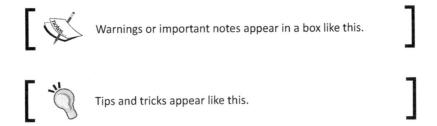

Downloading the example code

You can download the example code files for all Packt books you have purchased from your account at http://www.packtpub.com. If you purchased this book elsewhere, you can visit http://www.packtpub.com/support and register to have the files.e-mailed directly to you.

New terms and **important words** are shown in bold. Words that you see on the screen, in menus or dialog boxes for example, appear in the text like this: "clicking the **Next** button moves you to the next screen".

> Warnings or important notes appear in a box like this.

> Tips and tricks appear like this.

Reader feedback

Feedback from our readers is always welcome. Let us know what you think about this book—what you liked or may have disliked. Reader feedback is important for us to develop titles that you really get the most out of.

To send us general feedback, simply send an e-mail to feedback@packtpub.com, and mention the book title via the subject of your message.

If there is a topic that you have expertise in and you are interested in either writing or contributing to a book, see our author guide on www.packtpub.com/authors.

Customer support

Now that you are the proud owner of a Packt book, we have a number of things to help you to get the most from your purchase.

Downloading the example code

You can download the example code files for all Packt books you have purchased from your account at http://www.packtpub.com. If you purchased this book elsewhere, you can visit http://www.packtpub.com/support and register to have the files e-mailed directly to you.

Errata

Although we have taken every care to ensure the accuracy of our content, mistakes do happen. If you find a mistake in one of our books—maybe a mistake in the text or the code—we would be grateful if you would report this to us. By doing so, you can save other readers from frustration and help us improve subsequent versions of this book. If you find any errata, please report them by visiting http://www.packtpub.com/submit-errata, selecting your book, clicking on the **errata submission form** link, and entering the details of your errata. Once your errata are verified, your submission will be accepted and the errata will be uploaded on our website, or added to any list of existing errata, under the Errata section of that title. Any existing errata can be viewed by selecting your title from http://www.packtpub.com/support.

Piracy

Piracy of copyright material on the Internet is an ongoing problem across all media. At Packt, we take the protection of our copyright and licenses very seriously. If you come across any illegal copies of our works, in any form, on the Internet, please provide us with the location address or website name immediately so that we can pursue a remedy.

Please contact us at copyright@packtpub.com with a link to the suspected pirated material.

We appreciate your help in protecting our authors, and our ability to bring you valuable content.

Questions

You can contact us at questions@packtpub.com if you are having a problem with any aspect of the book, and we will do our best to address it.

1
Discovering Your Hidden Scripting Skills

Computer programming is viewed by the average person as requiring long periods of training to learn skills that are totally foreign, and darn near impossible to understand. The word geek is often used to describe a person that can write computer code. The perception is that learning to write code takes great technical skill that is just so hard to learn. This perception is totally unwarranted. You already have the skills needed but don't realize it. Together we will crush this false perception you may have of yourself by refocusing, one step at a time, the knowledge you already possess to write Unity scripts.

In this chapter we shall:

- Deal with preconceived fears and concepts about scripts
- See why we should use C# instead of UnityScript
- Introduce Unity's documentation for scripting
- Learn how Unity and the MonoDevelop editor work together

Let's begin our journey by eliminating any anxiety about writing scripts for Unity, and become familiar with our scripting environment.

Prerequisite knowledge for using this book

Great news if you are a scripting beginner! This book is for those with absolutely no knowledge of programming. It is devoted to teaching the basics of C# with Unity.

However, some knowledge of Unity's operation is required. I will only be covering the parts of the Unity interface that are related to writing C# code. I am assuming that you know your way around Unity's interface, how to work with GameObjects in your **Scene**, and how to locate **Components** and view their **Properties** in the **Inspector**.

Dealing with scriptphobia

You've got Unity up and running, studied the interface, added some GameObjects to the Scene. Now you're ready to have those GameObjects move around, listen, speak, pick up other objects, shoot the bad guys, or anything else you can dream of. So you click on Play, and nothing happens. Well darn it all anyway.

You just learned a big lesson, all those fantastic, highly detailed GameObjects are dumber than a hammer. They don't know anything, and they sure don't know how to do anything.

So you proceed to read the Unity forums, study some scripting tutorials, maybe even copy and paste some scripts to get some action going when you press Play. That's great, but then you realize you don't understand anything in the scripts you've copied. Sure, you probably recognize the words, but you fail to understand what those words do or mean in a script. It feels like gibberish.

You look at the code, your palms get sweaty, and you think to yourself, "Geez, I'll never be able to write scripts!" Perhaps you have **scriptphobia**: the fear of not being able to write instructions (I made that up). Is that what you have?

The fear that you cannot write down instructions in a coherent manner? You may believe you have this affliction, but you don't. You only think you do.

The basics of writing code are quite simple. In fact, you do things every day that are just like the steps executed in a script. For example, do you know how to interact with other people? How to operate a computer? Do you fret so much about making a baloney sandwich that you have to go to an online forum and ask how to do it?

Of course you don't. In fact, you know these things as "every day routines", or maybe as habits. Think for a moment, do you have to consciously think about these routines you do every day? Probably not. After you do them over and over, they become automatic.

The point is, you do things everyday following sequences of steps. Who created these steps you follow? More than likely you did, which means you've been scripting your whole life. You just never had to write down the steps, for your daily routines, on a piece of paper before doing them. You could write the steps down if you really wanted to, but it takes too much time and there's no need. But you do, in fact, know how to. Well, guess what? To write scripts, you only have to make one small change, start writing down the steps. Not for yourself but for the world you're creating in Unity.

So you see, you are already familiar with the concept of dealing with scripts. Most beginners to Unity easily learn their way around the Unity interface, how to add assets, and work in the Scene and Hierarchy windows. Their primary fear, and roadblock, is their false belief that scripting is too hard to learn.

Relax! You now have this book. I am going to get really basic in the beginning chapters. Call them baby-steps if you want, but you will see that scripting for Unity is similar to doing things you already do everyday. I'm sure you will have many "Ah-Ha" moments as you learn and overcome your unjustified fears and beliefs.

Teaching behaviors to GameObjects

You have Unity because you want to make a game or something interactive. You've filled your game full of dumb GameObjects. What you have to do now is be their teacher. You have to teach them everything they need to know to live in this make-believe world. This the part where you have to write down the instructions so that your GameObjects can be smarter.

Here's a quote from the Unity Manual:

> The **behavior** of GameObjects is controlled by the **Components** that are attached to them... Unity allows you to create your own **Components** using scripts.

Notice that word, behavior. It reminds me of a parent teaching a child proper behavior. This is exactly what we are going to do when we write scripts for our GameObjects, we're teaching them the behaviors we want them to have. The best part is, Unity has provided a big list of all the behaviors we can give to our GameObjects. This list of behaviors is documented in the Scripting Reference.

This means we can pick and chose, from this list of behaviors anything we want a GameObject to do. Unity has done all the hard work of programming all these behaviors for you. All we need to do is use a little code to tie into these behaviors. Did you catch that? Unity has already created the behaviors, all we have to do is supply a little bit of C# code to apply these behaviors to our GameObjects. Now really, how difficult can it be since Unity has already done most of the programming?

Choosing to use C# instead of UnityScript

So why choose C# to create this code? This maybe after-the-fact information for you if you've already acquired this book and chosen to use C#, but these are valuable points to know anyway:

Reason 1 for choosing C# – vast amount of documentation on the Internet

Have a look at the following bullet list, it will help you understand the reason for choosing C#:

- C# is a well known and a heavily used programming language developed by Microsoft for creating Windows application and web-based applications. If you ever need to know anything about C#, simply do a search on the Internet.

- UnityScript is just a scripting language designed specifically for Unity. It's similar to JavaScript, yet it isn't. You may be able to search for JavaScript solutions on the web, but the code may or may not work within the confines of Unity without modification, if at all.

- Why start off learning a limited scripting language, specific only to Unity, when you can use C#, a true programming language, and find information everywhere?

- Who knows, once you see how easy C# is, maybe you might decide to develop for Windows or the Web some day. You'll already have the basics of C#.

- Once you learn C#, you'll pretty much know UnityScript, too.

Reason 2 for choosing C# – flexibility to use Unity scripts and regular C# code files

- Any C# files you have in your Unity Project folder, that are not Unity scripts, are accessible without the need of attach them to GameObjects.

- The State Machine project we will create for this book makes use of C# code files that are not attached to any GameObject.

- I'm not saying you can't create a State Machine by using UnityScript. It's just so much easier with C#. Every UnityScript file has to be attached to a GameObject to work and be accessible to other scripts. C# overcomes this necessity.

Reason 3 for choosing C# – coding rules are specific

- ◆ C# is known as a strictly-typed language. What does this means to you?

- ◆ As you write code, Unity will catch coding errors immediately. Learning a subject is always easier when the rules are specific, and not some fuzzy "you can if you want to" kind of logic.

- ◆ UnityScript is not a strictly-typed language. You have the potential to write code that is not valid, but Unity won't catch the errors until you press Play.

- ◆ Finding mistakes as you write the code is so much easier than having to deal with them when a user has found them when they're playing the game.

- ◆ Please be aware, it is easy to force UnityScript to be strictly-typed, but if you're going to do that, then you may as well be using C# anyway, which brings us back to Reason 1.

Maneuvering around Unity's documentation

When we begin writing scripts, we will be looking at Unity's documentation quite often, so it's beneficial to know how to access the information we need. For an overview of a topic we'll use the **Reference Manual**. For specific coding details and examples we'll use the **Scripting Reference**.

When you look at the code examples in the **Scripting Reference**, they probably won't make sense to you, which is expected at this point. In the beginning chapters, as I teach you the basics of programming, it will be necessary for me to use a few things in the **Scripting Reference** such as displaying some output to Unity's **Console**. For now, just copy the code I use because you will be learning the detail of it later.

Time for action – opening the Reference Manual documentation for the transform Component

To get a feel for accessing Unity's documentation from within Unity, we'll use the **Main Camera** to demonstrate. Every GameObject in a Scene has a **Transform** Component, so we'll look at the documentation for **Transform** in the **Reference Manual** and the **Scripting Reference**. Getting to the information is pretty easy. Click on the tiny book icon with the question mark.

1. In the **Hierarchy** tab, select the **Main Camera**.

2. Click on the book icon for the **Transform**.

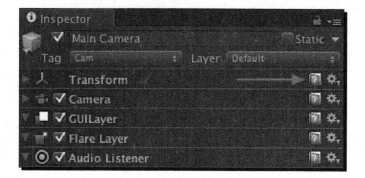

What just happened?

The web browser opened the **Reference Manual** showing information about Transform.

Time for action – opening the scripting reference documentation for the transform component

From the **Reference Manual**, we'll now open the **Scripting Reference** documentation for the **Transform Component**.

1. Click the link **Switch to Scripting** in the upper right-hand side of the browser window as shown in the following screenshot:

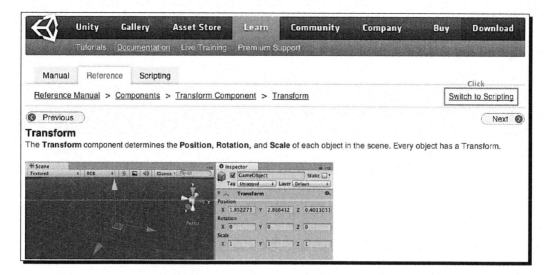

What just happened?

The **Transform** page in the **Scripting Reference** opens in the web browser as shown in the following screenshot:

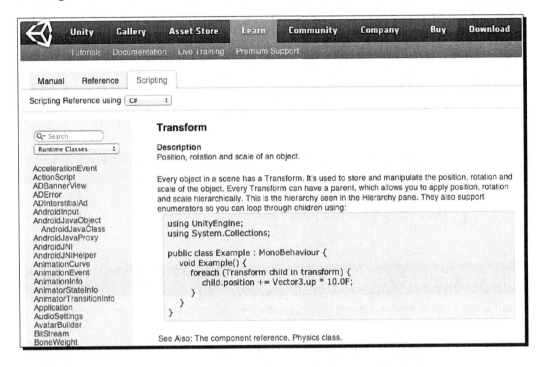

Are we really supposed to know all that stuff?

Actually, no. The whole reason for why the Scripting Reference exist is so we can look for information as we need it. Which will actually happen us to remember the code we do over and over, just like our other daily routines and habits.

What is all that information?

The previous screenshot shows a description and some sample code which probably doesn't mean much right now. Fear not! You'll eventually be able to look at that and say, "Hey, I know what that means!"

Working with C# script files

Until you learn some basic programming concepts, it's too early to study how scripts work, but we still need to know how to create one.

There are several ways to create a script file using Unity:

◆ In the menu navigate to **Assets | Create | C# Script**

Or

◆ In the **Project** tab navigate to **Create | C# Script**

Or

◆ In the **Project** tab right-click , from the pop-up menu navigate to **Create | C# Script**

 From now on, when I tell you to create a C# script, please use which ever method you prefer.

Time for action – create a C# script file

As our Unity project progresses, we will have several folders to organize and store all of our C# files.

1. Create a new Unity project and name it as `State Machine`.
2. Right-click on in the **Project** tab and create a folder named `Code`.
3. Right-click on the `Code` folder and a create a folder named `Scripts`.
4. In the `Scripts` folder, create a `C# Script`.
5. Immediately rename `NewBehaviourScript` to `LearningScript`.

What just happened?

We created one of the `Code` subfolders, named `Scripts`, that we will be using to organize our C# files. This folder will contain all of our Unity script files. Later we will create other C# file folders.

We also used Unity to create a C# script file named `LearningScript.cs`.

Introducing the MonoDevelop code editor

Unity uses an external editor to edit its C# scripts. Even though Unity can create a basic starter C# script for us, we still have to edit the script using the **MonoDevelop** code editor that's included with Unity.

Syncing C# files between MonoDevelop and Unity

Since Unity and MonoDevelop are separate applications, Unity will keep MonoDevelop and Unity synchronized with each other. This means that if you add, delete, or change a script file in one application, the other application will see the changes automatically.

Time for action – opening LearningScript in MonoDevelop

Unity will synchronize with MonoDevelop the first time you tell Unity to open a file for editing. The simplest way to do this is just double-click on LearningScript in the Scripts folder.

1. In Unity's Project tab, double-click on LearningScript:

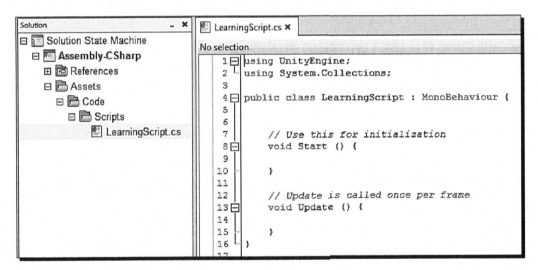

What just happened?

MonoDevelop started with LearningScript open, ready to edit.

Watching for a possible "gotcha" when creating script files in Unity

Notice line 4 in the previous screenshot:

```
public class LearningScript : MonoBehaviour
```

The class name `LearningScript` is the same as the file name `LearningScript.cs`. This is a requirement. You probably don't know what a class is yet, that's ok. Just remember that the file name and the class name must be the same.

When you create a C# script file in Unity, the filename, in the **Project** tab, is in Edit mode, ready to be renamed. Please rename it right then and there. If you rename the script later, the filename and the class name won't match. The filename would change, but line 4 would be this:

```
public class NewBehaviourScript : MonoBehaviour
```

This can easily be fixed in MonoDevelop by changing `NewBehaviourScript` on line 4 to the same name as the filename, but it's much simpler to do the renaming in Unity immediately.

Fixing sync if it isn't working properly

So what happens when Murphy's Law strikes and syncing just doesn't seem to be working correctly? Should the two apps somehow get out-of-sync as you switch back-and-forth between the them, for whatever reason, do this:

- Right-click on Unity's **Project** window and select **Sync MonoDevelop Project**. MonoDevelop will re-sync with Unity.

Pop quiz – dealing with scripts

Q1. As a beginner, what's the biggest obstacle to be overcome to be able to write C# code?

Q2. The Scripting Reference supplies example code and a short description of what the code does. What do you use to get full detailed descriptions of Unity's Components and features?

Q3. The Scripting Reference is a large document. How much it should you know before attempting to write any scripts?

Q4. When creating a script file in Unity, when is the best time to name the script file?

Summary

This chapter tried to put you at ease about writing scripts for Unity. You do have the ability to write down instructions which is all a script is, a sequence of instructions. We saw how simple it is to create a new script file. You probably create files on your computer all the time. We saw how to easily bring up Unity's documentation. Finally we had a look at the MonoDevelop editor. None of this was complicated. In fact, you probably use apps all the time that do similar things. Bottom line, there's nothing to fear here.

Alright, let's start off *Chapter 2, Introducing the Building Blocks for Unity Scripts by having an* introductory look at the building blocks of programming we'll be using: variables, methods, Dot Syntax, and the class. Don't let these terms scare you. The concepts behind each one of these are similar to things you do often, perhaps every day.

2
Introducing the Building Blocks for Unity Scripts

A programming language such as C# can appear to be very complicated at first but in reality, there are two parts that form its foundation. These parts are variables and methods. Therefore, understanding these critical parts is a prerequisite for learning any of the other features of C#. Being as critical as they are, they are very simple concepts to understand. Using these variable and method foundation pieces, we'll be introduced to the C# building blocks used to create Unity scripts.

For those people who get sweaty palms just thinking of the word script, wipe your hands and relax. In this chapter, I'm going to use terms that are already familiar to you to introduce the building blocks of programming. The following are the concepts introduced in this chapter:

- ◆ Using variables in a script
- ◆ Using methods in a script
- ◆ The class which is a container for variables and methods
- ◆ Turning a script into a Component
- ◆ Components communicating using the Dot Syntax

Let's have a look at these primary concepts.

Using the term method instead of function

You are constantly going to see the words **function** and **method** used everywhere as you learn Unity.

 The words function and method truly mean the same thing in Unity. They do the same thing.

Since you are studying C#, and C# is an **Object-Oriented Programming (OOP)** language, I will use the word "method" throughout this book, just to be consistent with C# guidelines. It makes sense to learn the correct terminology for C#. Also, UnityScript and Boo are OOP languages. The authors of the **Scripting Reference** probably should have used the word method instead of function in all documentation.

 From now on I'm going to use the words method or methods in this book. When I refer to the functions shown in the **Scripting Reference**, I'm going to use the word method instead, just to be consistent throughout this book.

Understanding what a variable does in a script

What is a variable? Technically, it's a tiny section of your computer's memory that will hold any information you put there. While a game runs, it keeps track of where the information is stored, the value kept there, and the type of the value. However, for this chapter, all you need to know is how a variable works in a script. It's very simple.

What's usually in a mailbox, besides air? Well, usually there's nothing but occasionally there is something in it. Sometimes there's money (a paycheck), bills, a picture from aunt Mabel, a spider, and so on. The point is what's in a mailbox can vary. Therefore, let's call each mailbox a variable instead.

Naming a variable

Using the picture of the country mailboxes, if I asked you to see what is in the mailbox, the first thing you'd ask is which one? If I said in the Smith mailbox, or the brown mailbox, or the round mailbox, you'd know exactly which mailbox to open to retrieve what is inside. Similarly, in scripts, you have to name your variables with a unique name. Then I can ask you what's in the variable named myNumber, or whatever cool name you might use.

A variable name is just a substitute for a value

As you write a script and make a variable, you are simply creating a placeholder or a substitute for the actual information you want to use. Look at the following simple math equation: 2 + 9 = 11

Simple enough. Now try the following equation: 11 + myNumber = ???

There is no answer to this yet. You can't add a number and a word. Going back to the mailbox analogy, write the number 9 on a piece of paper. Put it in the mailbox named myNumber. Now you can solve the equation. What's the value in myNumber? The value is 9. So now the equation looks normal: 11 + 9 = 20

The myNumber variable is nothing more than a named placeholder to store some data (information). So anywhere you would like the number 9 to appear in your script, just write myNumber, and the number 9 will be substituted.

Although this example might seem silly at first, variables can store all kinds of data that is much more complex than a simple number. This is just a simple example to show you how a variable works.

Time for action – creating a variable and seeing how it works

Let's see how this actually works in our script. Don't be concerned about the details of how to write this, just make sure your script is the same as the script shown in the next screenshot.

1. In the Unity **Project** panel, double-click on LearningScript.
2. In MonoDevelop, write the lines 6, 11, and 13 from the next screenshot.
3. Save the file.

```
1   using UnityEngine;
2   using System.Collections;
3
4   public class LearningScript : MonoBehaviour
5   {
6       public int myNumber = 9;
7
8       // Use this for initialization
9       void Start ()
10      {
11          Debug.Log(2 + 9);
12
13          Debug.Log(11 + myNumber);
14      }
15
16      // Update is called once per frame
17      void Update ()
18      {
19
20      }
21  }
```

To make this script work, it has to be attached to a GameObject. Currently, in our **State Machine** project we only have one GameObject, the **Main Camera**. This will do nicely since this script doesn't affect the **Main Camera** in any way. The script simply runs by virtue of it being attached to a GameObject.

1. Drag LearningScript onto the **Main Camera**.
2. Select **Main Camera** so that it appears in the **Inspector** panel.
3. Verify whether LearningScript is attached.
4. Open the Unity **Console** panel to view the output of the script.
5. Click on **Play**.

The preceding steps are shown in the following screenshot:

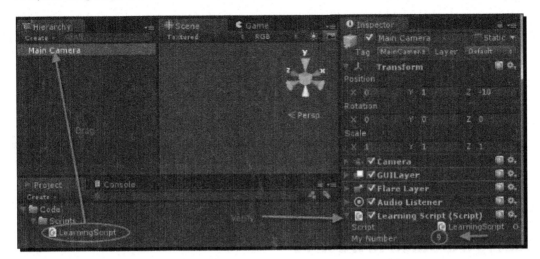

What just happened?

In the following **Console** panel is the result of our equations. As you can see, the equation on line 13 worked by substituting the number 9 for the myNumber variable:

Time for action – changing the number 9 to a different number

Since myNumber is a variable, the value it stores can vary. If we change what is stored in it, the answer to the equation will change too. Follow the ensuing steps:

1. Stop the game and change **9** to **19**.

2. Notice that when you restart the game, the answer will be **30**.

What just happened?

You learned that a variable works by simple process of substitution. There's nothing more to it than that.

We didn't get into the details of the wording used to create `myNumber`, or the types of variables you can create, but that wasn't the intent. This was just to show you how a variable works. It just holds data so you can use that data elsewhere in your script. We'll get into the finer details of variables in *Chapter 3, Variables in Detail*.

Have a go hero – changing the value of myNumber

In the **Inspector** panel, try changing the value of `myNumber` to some other value, even a negative value. Notice the change in answer in the **Console**.

Using a method in a script

Methods are where the action is and where the tasks are performed. Great, that's really nice to know but what is a method?

What is a method?

When we write a script, we are making lines of code that the computer is going to execute, one line at a time. As we write our code, there will be things we want our game to execute more than once. For example, we can write a code that adds two numbers. Suppose our game needs to add the two numbers together a hundred different times during the game. So you say, *"Wow, I have to write the same code a hundred times that adds two numbers together. There has to be a better way."*

Let a method take away your typing pain. You just have to write the code to add two numbers once, and then give this chunk of code a name, such as `AddTwoNumbers()`. Now, every time our game needs to add two numbers, don't write the code over and over, just call the `AddTwoNumbers()` method.

Time for action – learning how a method works

We're going to edit `LearningScript` again. In the following screenshot, there are a few lines of code that look strange. We are not going to get into the details of what they mean in this chapter. We will discuss that in *Chapter 4, Getting into the Details of Methods*. Right now, I am just showing you a method's basic structure and how it works:

1. In MonoDevelop, select `LearningScript` for editing.
2. Edit the file so that it looks exactly like the following screenshot.

3. Save the file.

```
1  using UnityEngine;
2  using System.Collections;
3
4  public class LearningScript : MonoBehaviour
5  {
6      public int number1 = 2;
7      public int number2 = 9;
8
9      void Start ()
10     {
11
12     }
13
14     void Update ()
15     {
16         if(Input.GetKeyUp(KeyCode.Return))
17             AddTwoNumbers();   ◄——— Calling the method
18     }
19
20     void AddTwoNumbers()
21     {
22         Debug.Log(number1 + number2);      The Method
23     }
24 }
```

What's in this script file?

In the previous screenshot, lines 6 and 7 will look familiar to you; they are variables just as you learned in the previous section. There are two of them this time. These variables store the numbers that are going to be added.

Line 16 may look very strange to you. Don't concern yourself right now with how this works. Just know that it's a line of code that lets the script know when the *Return/Enter* key is pressed. Press the *Return/Enter* key when you want to add the two numbers together.

Line 17 is where the AddTwoNumbers() method gets called into action. In fact, that's exactly how to describe it. This line of code calls the method.

Lines 20, 21, 22, and 23 make up the AddTwoNumbers() method. Don't be concerned about the code details yet. I just want you to understand how calling a method works.

Method names are substitutes too

You learned that a variable is a substitute for the value it actually contains. Well, a method is no different.

Take a look at line 20 from the previous screenshot:

```
void AddTwoNumbers ()
```

The AddTwoNumbers() is the name of the method. Like a variable, AddTwoNumbers() is nothing more than a named placeholder in the memory, but this time it stores some lines of code instead. So anywhere we would like to use the code of this method in our script, just write AddTwoNumbers(), and the code will be substituted.

Line 21 has an opening curly-brace and line 23 has a closing curly-brace. Everything between the two curly-braces is the code that is executed when this method is called in our script.

Look at line 17 from the previous screenshot:

```
AddTwoNumbers();
```

The method name AddTwoNumbers() is called. This means that the code between the curly-braces is executed.

 It's like having all of the code of a method right there on line 17.

Of course, this AddTwoNumbers() method only has one line of code to execute, but a method could have many lines of code.

Line 22 is the action part of this method, the part between the curly-braces. This line of code is adding the two variables together and displaying the answer to the Unity **Console**. Then, follow the ensuing steps:

1. Go back to Unity and have the **Console** panel showing.
2. Now click on **Play**.

What just happened?

Oh no! Nothing happened!

Actually, as you sit there looking at the blank **Console** panel, the script is running perfectly, just as we programmed it. Line 16 in the script is waiting for you to press the *Return/Enter* key. Press it now.

And there you go! The following screenshot shows you the result of adding two variables together that contain the numbers 2 and 9:

Line 16 waited for you to press the *Return/Enter* key. When you do this, line 17 executes which calls the `AddTwoNumbers()` method. This allows the code block of the method, line 23, to add the the values stored in the variables `number1` and `number2`.

Have a go hero – changing the output of the method

While Unity is in the **Play** mode, select the **Main Camera** so its Components show in the **Inspector**. In the **Inspector** panel, locate **Learning Script** and its two variables. Change the values, currently **2** and **9**, to different values. Make sure to click your mouse in the **Game** panel so it has focus, then press the *Return/Enter* key again. You will see the result of the new addition in the **Console**.

You just learned how a method works to allow a specific block of code to to be called to perform a task.

We didn't get into any of the wording details of methods here, this was just to show you fundamentally how they work. We'll get into the finer details of methods in *Chapter 4, Getting into the Details of Methods*.

Introducing the class

The **class** plays a major role in Unity. In fact, what Unity does with a class a little piece of magic when Unity creates Components.

You just learned about variables and methods. These two items are the building blocks used to build Unity scripts. The term script is used everywhere in discussions and documents. Look it up in the dictionary and it can be generally described as written text. Sure enough, that's what we have. However, since we aren't just writing a screenplay or passing a note to someone, we need to learn the actual terms used in programming.

Unity calls the code it creates a C# script. However, people like me have to teach you some basic programming skills and tell you that a script is really a class.

 In the previous section about methods, we created a class (script) called `LearningScript`. It contained a couple of variables and a method. The main concept or idea of a class is that it's a container of data, stored in variables, and methods that process that data in some fashion. Because I don't have to constantly write class (script), I will be using the word script most of the time. However, I will also be using class when getting more specific with C#. Just remember that a script is a class that is attached to a GameObject.

In *Chapter 7, Creating the Gameplay is Just a Part of the Game*, we will be creating some classes for a State Machine. These classes will not be attached to any GameObjects, so I won't be calling them scripts.

By using a little Unity magic, a script becomes a Component

While working in Unity, we wear the following two hats:

◆ A Game-Creator hat

◆ A Scripting (programmer) hat

When we first wear our Game-Creator hat, we will be developing our Scene, selecting GameObjects, and viewing Components; just about anything except writing our scripts.

When we put our Scripting hat on, our terminology changes as follows:

◆ We're writing code in scripts using MonoDevelop

◆ We're working with variables and methods

The magic happens when you put your Game-Creator hat back on and attach your script to a GameObject. Wave the magic wand — ZAP — the script file is now called a Component, and the public variables of the script are now the properties you can see and change in the **Inspector** panel.

A more technical look at the magic

A script is like a blueprint or a written description. In other words, it's just a single file in a folder on our hard drive. We can see it right there in the **Projects** panel. It can't do anything just sitting there. When we tell Unity to attach it to a GameObject, we haven't created another copy of the file, all we've done is tell Unity we want the behaviors described in our script to be a Component of the GameObject.

When we click on the **Play** button, Unity loads the GameObject into the computer's memory. Since the script is attached to a GameObject, Unity also has to make a place in the computer's memory to store a Component as part of the GameObject. The Component has the capabilities specified in the script (blueprint) we created.

Even more Unity magic

There's some more magic you need to be aware of. The scripts inherit from
`MonoBehaviour`.

For beginners to Unity, studying C# inheritance isn't a subject you need to learn in any great
detail, but you do need to know that each Unity script uses inheritance. We see the code in
every script that will be attached to a GameObject. In `LearningScript`, the code is on line 4:

```
public class LearningScript : MonoBehaviour
```

The colon and the last word of that code means that the `LearningScript` class is inheriting
behaviors from the `MonoBehaviour` class. This simply means that the MonoBehaviour
class is making few of its variables and methods available to the LearningScript class. It's
no coincidence that the variables and methods inherited look just like some of the code
we saw in the **Unity Scripting Reference**.

The following are the two inherited behaviors in the `LearningScript`:

Line 9:: `void Start ()`

Line 14: `void Update ()`

 The magic is that you don't have to call these methods, Unity calls them
automatically. So the code you place in these methods gets executed automatically.

Have a go hero – finding Start and Update in the Scripting Reference

Try a search on the **Scripting Reference** for **Start** and **Update** to learn when each method is
called by Unity and how often.

Also search for `MonoBehaviour`. This will show you that since our script inherits from
`MonoBehaviour`, we are able to use the `Start()` and `Update()` methods.

Components communicating using the Dot Syntax

Our script has variables to hold data, and our script has methods to allow tasks to be
performed. I now want to introduce the concept of communicating with other GameObjects
and the Components they contain. Communication between one GameObject's Components
and another GameObject's Components using Dot Syntax is a vital part of scripting. It's
what makes interaction possible. We need to communicate with other Components or
GameObjects to be able to use the variables and methods in other Components.

What's with the dots?

When you look at the code written by others, you'll see words with periods separating them. What the heck is that? It looks complicated, doesn't it. The following is an example from the Unity documentation:

```
transform.position.x
```

 Don't concern yourself with what the preceding code means as that comes later, I just want you to see the dots.

That's called the Dot Syntax. The following is another example. It's the fictitious address of my house: USA.Vermont.Essex.22MyStreet

Looks funny, doesn't it? That's because I used the syntax (grammar) of C# instead of the post office. However, I'll bet if you look closely, you can easily figure out how to find my house. We'll get into much more Dot Syntax detail in *Chapter 6, Using Dot Syntax for Object Communication*.

Pop quiz – knowing the C# building blocks

Q1. What is the purpose of a variable in a script?

Q2. What is the purpose of a method in a script?

Q3. How does a script become a Component?

Q4. What is the purpose of Dot Syntax?

Summary

This chapter introduced you to the basic concepts of variables, methods, and Dot Syntax. These building blocks are used to create scripts and classes. Understanding how these building blocks work is critical so you don't feel you're not getting it.

We discovered that a variable name is a substitute for the value it stores; a method name is a substitute for a block of code; when a script or class is attached to a GameObject, it becomes a Component. The Dot Syntax is just like an address to locate GameObjects and Components.

With these concepts under your belt, we can proceed to learn the details of the sentence structure, the grammar, and the syntax used to work with variables, methods, and the Dot Syntax. In the next chapter we will learn about the details of using variables.

3
Getting into the Details of Variables

Initially, computer programming appears difficult to beginners due to the fact how words are used in code. It's not the actual words that cause the problem because, for the most part, many of the words are the same words that we use in our everyday life. C# is not a foreign language. The main problem is that the words simply don't read like the typical sentences we are all used to. You know how to say the words and you know how to spell the words. What you don't know is where and why you need to put them in that crazy looking grammar, that is, the syntax that makes up a C #statement.

In this chapter, we will learn some of the basic rules for writing a C# statement. We will also be introduced to many of the words that C# uses and the proper placement of these words in the C# statements when we create our variables.

In this chapter we will cover the following topics:

- Writing C# statements properly
- Using C# syntax to write variable statements
- The GameObject Component's properties
- Using public variables for the Unity Inspector panel
- Naming a variable properly
- Declaring a variable for the type of data it will store

Ok, let's learn some programming grammar, otherwise known as C# syntax.

Writing C# statements properly

When you do normal writing, it's in the form of a sentence with a period used to end the sentence. When you write a line of code, it's called a statement with a semi-colon used to end the statement.

 The reason a statement ends with a semi-colon is so that Unity knows when the statement ends. A period can't be used because they are used in the Dot Syntax.

The code for a C# statement does not have to be on a single line as shown in the following example:

```
public int number1 = 2;
```

The statement can be on several lines. Whitespace and carriage returns are ignored, so if you really want to, you can write it as follows:

```
public
int
number1
=
2;
```

But I recommend you to not write your code like this because it's terrible reading code formatted like the preceding code. However, there will be times that you'll have to write long statements that will be longer than one line. Unity won't care. It just needs to see the semi-colon at the end.

Understanding Component properties in Unity's Inspector

GameObjects have some Components that make them behave in a certain way. For instance, select **Main Camera** and look at the **Inspector** panel. One of the Components is the **Camera**. Without that Component, it will cease being a camera. It would still be a GameObject in your scene, just no longer a functioning camera.

Variables become Component properties

Any Component of any GameObject is just a script that defines a class, whether you wrote the script or the Unity's programmer did. We just aren't supposed to edit the scripts that Unity wrote. This means that all the properties we see in **Inspector** are just variables of some type. They simply store data that will be used by some methods.

Unity changes script and variable names slightly

When we add our script to a GameObject, the name of our script shows up in the **Inspector** panel as a Component. Unity makes a couple of small changes. You might have noticed that when we added `LearningScript` to **Main Camera**, Unity actually showed it in the **Inspector** panel as **Learning Script**. Unity added a space to separate the words of the name. Unity does this modification to the variable names, too. Notice that the variable `number1` is shown as **Number 1**, and `number2` as **Number 2**. Unity capitalizes the first letter as well. These displayed changes improve readability in **Inspector**.

Changing a property's value in the Inspector panel

There are two situations when you can modify a property value:

- During the **Play** mode
- During the development mode (not in the **Play** mode)

When you are in the **Play** mode, you will see that your changes take effect immediately in real time. This is great when you're experimenting and want to see the results.

When you are in the **Play** mode, you will see that your changes take effect immediately in real time. This is great when you're experimenting and want to see the results. Write down any changes you want to keep because when you stop the **Play** mode, any changes you made will be lost.

When you are in the development mode, changes you make to the property values will be saved by Unity. This means that if you quit Unity and restart it again, the changes will be retained. Of course you won't see the effect of your change until you click on **Play**.

The changes you make to the property values in the **Inspector** panel do not modify your script. The only way your script can be changed is for you to edit it in the script editor (MonoDevelop). The values shown in the **Inspector** panel override any values you had assigned in your script.

If you desire to undo the changes you've made in the **Inspector** panel, you can reset the values to the default values assigned in your script. Click on the Cog icon (the gear) on the far right of the Component script, and then select **Reset** as shown in the following screenshot:

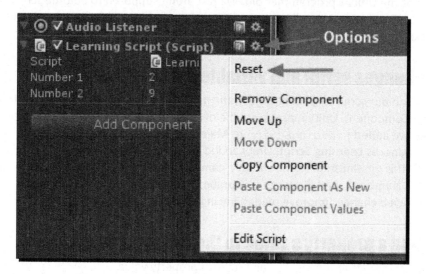

Displaying public variables in the Inspector panel

I'm sure you're wondering what the word `public` means at the beginning of a variable statement:

```
public int number1 = 2;
```

It means that the variable will be visible and accessible. It will be visible as a property in the **Inspector** panel so that you can manipulate the value stored in the variable. It also means it can be accessed from other scripts using the Dot Syntax. You'll learn more about the Dot Syntax in *Chapter 6, Using Dot Syntax for Object Communication*.

Time for action – making a variable private

Not all variables need to be `public`. If there's no need for a variable to be changed in the **Inspector** panel nor be accessed from other scripts, it doesn't make sense to clutter the **Inspector** panel with needless properties. In `LearningScript`, perform the following steps:

1. Change line 6 to the following:

```
private int number1 = 2;
```

2. Change line 7 to the following:

```
int number2 = 9;
```

3. Save the file.

4. In Unity, select **Main Camera**.

What just happened?

You will notice in the **Inspector** panel that both properties, **Number 1** and **Number 2** are gone.

- Line 6: `private int number1 = 2;`

    The preceding line explicitly states that the `number1` variable is to be `private`, therefore the variable is no longer a property in the **Inspector** panel. It is now a private variable to store data.

- Line 7: `int number2 = 9;`

    The `number2` variable is no longer visible as a property either, but you didn't specify it as `private`.

If you don't explicitly state whether a variable will be `public` or `private`, by default, the variable will implicitly be `private`.

 It is good coding practice to explicitly state whether a variable will be `public` or `private`.

So now when you click on **Play**, the script works exactly as it did before. You just can't manipulate the values manually in the **Inspector** panel anymore.

Naming your variables properly

Always use meaningful names for storing your variables. If you don't do that, six months down the line, you will be sad. I'm going to exaggerate here a little bit to make a point. I will name a variable as shown in the following code:

```
public bool theBearMakesBigPottyInTheWoods = true;
```

That's a descriptive name. In other words, you know what it means by just reading the variable, and so ten years from now when you look at that name, you'll know exactly what it means. Now suppose instead of `theBearMakesBigPottyInTheWoods`, I had named this variable as shown in the following code:

```
public bool potty = true;
```

Sure, you know what `potty` is, but would you know that it referred to a bear making a big potty in the woods? I know right now you'll understand it because you just wrote it, but six months down the line, after writing hundreds of other scripts for all sorts of different projects, you'll look at that and wonder what `potty` meant. You'll have to read several lines of code you wrote to try to figure it out.

You may look at the code and wonder who in their right mind would write such a terrible code. So take the time to write a descriptive code that even a stranger can look at and know what you mean. Believe me, in six months or probably less, you will be that stranger.

Begin variable names with lowercase

You should begin a variable name with lowercase because it helps to distinguish between a class name and a variable name in your code. The Component names (class names) begin with a capital letter. For example, it's easy to know that `Transform` is a class, and `transform` is a variable.

There are of course exceptions to this general rule, and every programmer has a preferred way to use lowercase, uppercase, and perhaps an underscore to begin a variable name. At the end, you will have to decide upon a naming convention you like. If you read the Unity forums, there are some heated debates on naming variables. In this book, I will show you my preferred way, but you can use whatever is more comfortable for you.

Using multi-word variable names

Let's use the same example again as follows:

```
public bool theBearMakesBigPottyInTheWoods = true;
```

You can see that the variable name is actually eight words squished together. Since variable names can be only one word, begin the first word with a lowercase, and then just capitalize the first letter of each additional word. It greatly helps to create descriptive names and still being able to read it. There's a word for this called **camelCasing**.

Have a go hero – viewing multi-word variables in the Inspector panel

I already mentioned that for `public` variables, Unity's **Inspector** will separate each word and capitalize the first word. Go ahead, add the previous statement to `LearningScript` and see what Unity does with it in the **Inspector** panel.

Declaring a variable and its type

Every variable we want to use in a script must be declared in a statement. What does that mean? Well, before Unity can use a variable; we have to tell Unity about it first. Ok then, what are we supposed to tell Unity about the variable?

There are only three absolute requirements for declaring a variable and they are as follows:

- ◆ We have to specify the type of data a variable can store
- ◆ We have to provide a name for the variable
- ◆ We have to end the declaration statement with a semi-colon

The following is the syntax we use for declaring a variable:

```
typeOfData nameOfTheVariable;
```

Let's use one of the `LearningScript` variables as an example; the following is how to declare a variable with the bare minimum requirements:

```
int number1;
```

The following is what we have:

- ◆ **Requirement #1** is the type of data that `number1` can store, which in this case is an `int`, meaning an integer
- ◆ **Requirement #2** is a name which is `number1`
- ◆ **Requirement #3** is the semi-colon at the end

The second requirement of naming a variable has already been discussed. The third requirement of ending a statement with a semi-colon has been discussed. The first requirement of specifying the type of data will be covered next.

The following is what we know about this bare minimum declaration as far as Unity is concerned:

- ◆ There's no `public` modifier which means it's `private` by default
- ◆ It won't appear in the **Inspector** panel, or be accessible from other scripts
- ◆ The value stored in `number1` defaults to zero

The most common built-in variable types

This section only shows the most common built-in types of data that C# provides for us and that variables can store.

Just these basic types are presented here so that you understand the concept of a variable being able to store only the type of the data you specify. The custom types of data that you will create later will be discussed in *Chapter 7, Creating the Gameplay is Just a Part of the Game* in the discussion of Dot Syntax.

The following chart shows the most common built-in types of data you will use in Unity:

Type	Contents of the variable
int	A simple integer, such as the number 3
float	A number with a decimal, such as the number 3.14
string	Characters in double quotes, such as, "Watch me go now"
bool	A boolean, either **true** or **false**

There are few more built-in types of data that aren't shown in the preceding chart. However, once you understand the most common types, you'll have no problem looking up the other built-in types if you ever need to use them.

We know the minimum requirements to declare a variable. However, we can add more information to a declaration to save our time and coding. We've already seen some examples in `LearningScript` of assigning values when the variable is being declared and now we'll see few more examples.

Time for action – assigning values while declaring the variable

Add some more variables to `LearningScript` using the types shown in the previous chart. While declaring the variables, assign them values as shown in the following screenshot. See how they are presented in the **Inspector** panel. These are all `public` variables so they will appear in the **Inspector** panel:

```
1   using UnityEngine;
2   using System.Collections;
3
4   public class LearningScript : MonoBehaviour
5   {
6       public int number1 = 2;
7       public float number2 = 4.7f;
8       public string someWords = "Now is the time";
9       public bool checkThisOut = true;
10
11      void Start ()
12      {
13
14      }
15
16      void Update ()
17      {
18
19      }
```

What just happened?

The following screenshot shows what Unity presents in the **Inspector** panel:

The variables are displayed in the **Inspector** panel with the values already set.

Where you declare a variable is important

You will be declaring and using variables in many places in a script. The variables that I have shown you so far are called **member variables**. They are members of the LearningScript class, not declared within any method. These member variables are the only variables that have the option of being displayed in the **Inspector** panel or being accessed by other scripts.

So where in the class should the member variables be declared? This is another subject that can lead to heated discussions. Personally, I declare them at the top of a class file before any methods are declared so that I see them all in one place. Other people like to declare variables close to the point of first use in a method.

Declaring your member variables at the beginning of a class may give you a mental clue that these member variables can be used everywhere in the script.

We will also be creating variables in methods. These variables are called as **local variables** and are never displayed in the Unity's **Inspector** panel, nor can they be accessed by other scripts. This brings us to another programming concept called **variable scope**.

Variable scope – determining where a variable can be used

Variable scope is a fancy way of saying "Where in the script does a variable exist". The following screenshot explains you the scope of variables:

```
1   using UnityEngine;
2   using System.Collections;
3
4   public class LearningScript : MonoBehaviour
5   {
6       string block1 = "Block 1 text";          Code Block 1
7
8       void Start ()
9       {
10          Debug.Log(block1);                    Code Block 2
11          string block2 = "Block 2 text";
12          Debug.Log(block2);
13          {
14              Debug.Log(block1);                Code Block 3
15              Debug.Log(block2);
16              string block3 = "Block 3 text";
17              Debug.Log(block3);
18          }
19       }
20   }
21
```

You might have noticed that the rectangular blocks start and end with curly-braces. Just like the `AddTwoNumbers()` method in *Chapter 2, Introducing the Building blocks for Unity Scripts*, the code between the opening curly-brace and a closing curly-brace is called a **code block**. Absolutely anywhere in a code that you have an opening curly-brace, there will be a closing curly-brace to match. All the code between the two braces is a code block.

Notice that the code blocks can be nested inside other code blocks.

 You normally don't just create bare blocks of code with curly-braces like I did with **Code Block 3**. Code blocks are usually part of other things such as if statements, looping statements, and methods. This example is just to demonstrate how the scope of a variable works, and where a variable exists and is useable.

The following is what you have:

Line 16: `string block3 = "Block 3 text";`

The preceding line declares a local `string` variable named `block3`. This variable exists in the code block that is labeled **Code Block 3**. If you try to use the variable `block3` outside of **Code Block 3**, such as in **Code Block 2** or **Code Block 1**, Unity will give you an error message saying that variable `block3` doesn't exist.

The scope of the variable `block3` is the code block defined by the curly-braces of lines 13 and 18.

Now let's look at the `block1` variable:

Line 6: `string block1 = "Block 1 text";`

The preceding line declares a `string` type member variable named `block1`. This variable exists in the code block that is labeled **Code Block 1**. This code block begins on line 5 and ends on line 20. This means the variable `block1` can be used everywhere, including **Code Block 2 and Code Block 3** because, they are also within **Code Block 1**. The `block1` variable is used in **Code Block 2** on line 10, and in **Code Block 3** on line 14.

The scope of the `block1` variable is the code block defined by the curly-braces between lines 5 and 20.

Pop quiz – knowing how to declare a variable

Q1. What is the proper way to name a variable?

Q2. How do you make a variable appear in the Unity's **Inspector** panel?

Q3. Can all variables in a script show in the **Inspector** panel?

Q4. Can a variable store any type of data?

Summary

We first covered how to write a C# statement, especially the semi-colon to terminate a statement. All the Component properties shown in the **Inspector** panel are member variables in the Component's class. Member variables can be shown in the **Inspector** panel, or accessed by other scripts when the variable is declared as `public`. The type of data a variable can store is specified when it's declared. Finally, we learned that variable scope determines where it is allowed to be used.

Now that we've learned about variables, we're ready to learn the details of C# methods that will use the variables we create – which is the topic of the next chapter.

4

Getting into the Details of Methods

In the previous chapter, you were introduced to a variable's scope—where a variable exists and is allowed to be used. The scope is determined by the "opening" and "closing" curly braces. The purpose of those curly braces is to act as a container for a block of executable code, a code block. In second chapter you saw that a method is a code block that can execute by just calling the method's name. It's time to see the importance of code blocks and the variables used in them. A method defines a code block which begins and ends with curly braces.

In this chapter we will cover the features of methods:

- Ending method definitions with curly braces
- Using methods in a script
- Naming methods properly
- Defining a method
- Calling a method
- Returning a value from a method
- Using Unity's `Update()` and `Start()` methods

Variables are the first major building block of C#, methods are the second, so let's dive into methods.

Ending a method definition using curly braces

At the beginning of *Chapter 3*, *Getting into the Details of Variables* you learned about C# statements and the requirement to end them with a semicolon. A method definition has a different requirement.

A method definition ends with a code block between a pair of curly braces. *DO NOT* end a method definition with a semicolon.

If you do accidentally place a semicolon at the end, MonoDevelop will gladly remind you with an error message that you're not supposed to use a semicolon at the end of a method definition.

Using methods in a script

There are two reasons for using methods in a script:

◆ To provide behavior to a GameObject

◆ To create reusable sections of code

 All of the executable code in a script is in methods.

The first purpose of a method is to work with the member variables of the class. The member variables store data that's needed for a Component to give a GameObject its behavior. The whole reason for writing a script is to make a GameObject do something interesting. A method is the place we make the behavior come to life.

The second purpose of a method is to create code blocks that will be used over and over again. You don't want to be writing the same code over and over. Instead, you place the code into a code block and give it a name so you can call it when needed.

Naming methods properly

Always use meaningful names for your methods. Just like I explained for variables, if you don't use good names, then six months from now you will be sad.

Since methods make GameObject do something useful, you should give your method a name that sounds like "action." For example, `JumpOverTheFence` or `ClimbTheWall`. You can look at those names and know exactly what the method is going to do.

Don't make them too simple. Suppose you name a method `Wiggle`. Sure you know what Wiggle means right now, but in six months you'll look at that and say "Wiggle? Wiggle what?" It only takes a moment to be a little more precise and write `WiggleMyButt`. Now when you see that method name, you'll know exactly what it's going to do.

Begin method names with an uppercase letter

Why? We do this to make it easier to tell the difference between what is a class or method, and what is a variable. Also, Microsoft suggests beginning **method names** with an **uppercase** letter. If someone else ever looks at your code, they will expect to see **method names** beginning with an **uppercase** letter.

Using multi-word names for a method

Using this example again:

```
void AddTwoNumbers ()
{
  // Code goes here
}
```

You can see the name is actually three words squished together. Since method names can only one word, the first word begins uppercase, then just capitalize the first letter of each additional word. For example, PascalCasing.

Parentheses are part of the method name

The method name always includes a pair of parentheses on the end. The parentheses not only let you know that the name is a method, but they do serve an important purpose of allowing you to input some data into the method when needed.

Defining a method properly

Just like for variables, we have to let Unity know about a method before we can use it.

Depending on who you talk to, some will say we have to **declare** a method, others will say we have to **define** a method. Which is correct? In C#, it doesn't make any difference. Use which ever term helps you learn easier. I like to say I'm **defining** a method's code block, nothing like **declaring** a simple variable on a one line statement.

The minimum requirements for defining a method

There are three minimum requirements for defining a method:

- The type of information, or data, a method will return to the place where the method was called

- The name of the method should be followed by a pair of parentheses

- A pair of curly braces should be present for containing the code block:

```
returnDataType    NameOfTheMethod ( )
{
}
```

Looking at `LearningScript` once again, or any Unity generated script, the `Start()` method has the three bare-bone minimum requirements for a method:

```
void Start ()
{
}
```

Here's what we have:

- Our first requirement is the type of data the method will return to the place in the code that called this method. This method isn't returning any value, so instead of specifying an actual type of data, the keyword `void` is used. This informs Unity that nothing is being returned from the method.

- Second requirement is the method name which is `Start()`.

- Last requirement is the curly braces, which contains the code that defines what the method is going to do.

This example fulfills the bare minimum requirements to be a method. However, as you can see, there's no code in the code block, so when `Start()` is called by Unity, it doesn't do anything at all, but it's still a method. Normally, if we aren't going to use a method by adding code to a skeleton method created by Unity, we can simply remove them from our script. It's normally best to remove unused code after the script is done being written.

Here's what we know about this bare minimum method definition as far as Unity is concerned:

- There's no public modifier, which means this method is `private` by default. Therefore, this method cannot be called from other scripts.

- There's no code in the code block. Therefore, this method doesn't do anything, so it can be removed if we wish.

Understanding parentheses – why are they there?

One thing for sure is that it makes easy to recognize that it's a method, but why are they part of a method's name?

We already know that a method is a code block that is going to get called multiple times. That's one of the reasons why a method created in the first place, so we don't have to write the same code over and over. Remember the AddTwoNumbers () method back in Chapter 2. It was very simple method used to explain the concept of a method and how to call it. Now it's time to take the next step and learn the usefulness of the parentheses.

Time for action – adding code between the parentheses

We're going to modify `LearningScript` to send some information to the `AddTwoNumbers()` method to make it much more useful.

Why would we need to send information to a method?

A script may need to add two numbers several times, but they probably won't always be the same two numbers. We could possibly have hundreds of different combinations of "two numbers" to add together. This means that we need to let the method know, which two numbers need to be added together at the moment when we call the method.

```
1  using UnityEngine;
2  using System.Collections;
3
4  public class LearningScript : MonoBehaviour
5  {
6      int number1 = 2;
7      int number2 = 3;
8      int number3 = 7;
9
10     void Start ()
11     {
12         AddTwoNumbers(number1, number2);
13         AddTwoNumbers(number1, number3);
14         AddTwoNumbers(number2, number3);
15     }
16
17     void Update ()
18     {
19
20     }
21
22     void AddTwoNumbers (int firstNumber, int secondNumber)
23     {
24         int result = firstNumber + secondNumber;
25         Debug.Log(result);
26     }
27 }
28
```

Using the preceding screenshot, perform the following steps:

1. Open `LearningScript` in MonoDevelop to modify it.
2. Add lines 6, 7, and 8 to declare three integer variables.
3. Add lines 22 to 26 to define the `AddTwoNumbers()` method with parameters.
4. Add lines 12, 13, and 14 to call the `AddTwoNumbers()` three times.
5. Save the file.
6. Click on **Play** in Unity.

What just happened?

As this script executes, the `AddTwoNumbers()` method is called three times on lines 12, 13, and 14. The method's code block adds two numbers and displays the result in the Unity **Console** (see the yellow arrows in the following screenshot):

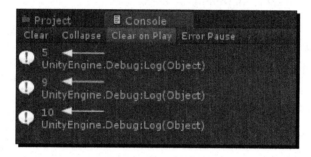

Those parentheses are like a *cubbyhole*. When we call `AddTwoNumbers()` a couple of numbers are stuffed into the cubbyhole. When the code block executes, it takes those two numbers held in the cubbyhole and uses them on line 24.

There's a special name for that information between the parentheses of a method definition, such as line 22—the code is called the method parameters.

Specifying a method's parameters

If you look up the word parameters in the dictionary, your brain will probably seize up. All it means is that the method has to be able to use the information you send it, so you simply have to specify the type of data the method is allowed to use. That's it, it's very simple.

In the earlier screenshot, on line 22 the red arrows pointed to the type of the declared variables `firstNumber` and `secondNumber`. The type is `int`, or `integer`. Now notice the red arrow pointing to the variables `number1`, `number2`, and `number3`. They are also of the type `int`. These variables have to be of type `int` since they store the numbers that will be added in the method, which the parameters specify will be of type `int`.

So now go look in the dictionary again. You will probably see the word limit in there somewhere. That's what you did when you specified the type of data, an integer, that the method will use. You set some limits on what's allowed.

Ok, so you're setting parameters, or limits, on the type of data the method can use, but what exactly is a parameter? Well, the first parameter is called `firstNumber`, and what is `firstNumber` doing? It's storing a value that will be used in the code block on line 24. What do we call things that store data? That's right, variables. Variables are used everywhere.

 Remember, a variable is just a substitute name for the value it actually stores.

As you can see on line 22 of the code block, those variables are being added together.

How many parameters can a method have?

We can have as many as you need to make the method work properly. Whether we write our own custom methods, or you use the methods of the scripting reference, the parameters that are defined are what the method will require to be able to perform its specified task.

Calling a method

In the earlier screenshot, look at lines 12 and 22. Do you notice anything different? They sure don't look the same, do they? The variable names, which the blue arrows point to, are different.

If you are looking at that code and saying "What the heck?" then don't feel bad. When I was first learning the concept of calling methods, I had one heck of time understanding how the code worked. It is, in fact, very simple, but I fought with this for days before the lights came on. I consulted all the programming books I had, written by all the experts, and not a single one had the decency to explain how the code worked. All those book authors just assumed I'd "get it" because after all, they were experts.

I had to figure it out myself with trial and error testing. After many days, I finally had my "Ah-Ha" moment.

Using arguments in the parentheses of a method

Arguments?? Who dreams up these words? We all know what an argument is. Every one of us has been involved in an argument at some time. Well, someone decided this would be a good word to mean something in programming. Sure enough, look it up in a dictionary and you'll probably see something like this: "A value or address passed to a procedure or function at the time of call."

Yup, that explains it totally, right? Ok, let's really learn what arguments are, and what they do in code. In the previous screenshot, look at line 12:

```
AddTwoNumbers(number1, number2);
```

Between the parentheses are the variables, `number1` and `number2`. Those two variables are called the arguments that are being passed to the method. In simple terms, the values stored in these two variables, 2 and 3, are placed in the cubbyhole.

On line 22, the method defines that it takes in two parameters called `firstNumber` and `secondNumber`. This means, of course, that somewhere in this process these parameters will have to have values assigned them.

Here's the secret I finally discovered on my own. Behind the scenes, where you can't see, the values 2 and 3, that are in the cubbyhole, are now assigned to the variables `firstNumber` and `secondNumber`.

You don't see this code, but if you could see it, what happens with arguments and parameters looks just like this:

```
firstNumber = number1;
secondNumber = number2;
```

- Since the argument `number1` contained the value 2, now the parameter `firstNumber` contains the value 2
- Since the argument `number2` contained the value 3, now the parameter `secondNumber` contains the value 3

Now the code block is executed and the value 5 is displayed in the Unity **Console**.

As you can now see, the names of the arguments and the names of the parameters don't need to be the same. They're just names of variables used in different places in your code. They're just substitutes for the actual values each contain, and it's the value that's getting transferred from the method call to the method code block.

Returning a value from a method

Now it's time to discover the "power" feature of using a method. This usually means sending data to the method, which you just learned to do, then have the method return a value back. Previously, all you had the `AddTwoNumbers()` method do was take the result of adding two numbers and display it to Unity's Console.

Now, instead of displaying the result directly, you're going to modify `AddTwoNumbers()` to return the result of the addition back to the place the method was called.

Remember, I told you that when you call a method, it's just a substitute for the code block that will be executed. It's like taking all the code in the method's code block and placing it right there where the method was called.

The next screenshot is still very simple, but it shows how this substitution works and how returning a value from a method works.

Time for action – returning a value from AddTwoNumbers()

Modify LearningScript to call the AddTwoNumbers() method twice and get a grand total. Also create another method whose sole purpose is to display the grand total result.

1. Open LearningScript in MonoDevelop to modify it.

2. On line 12, declare the answer variable (this statement is on 3 lines).

3. On lines 19 to 23, redefine the AddTwoNumbers() method with a return type.

4. On lines 25 to 28, define the DisplayResult() method.

5. Save the file.

6. Click on Play in Unity.

```
1  using UnityEngine;
2  using System.Collections;
3
4  public class LearningScript : MonoBehaviour
5  {
6      int number1 = 2;
7      int number2 = 3;
8      int number3 = 7;
9
10     void Start ()
11     {                          Notice this single statement is on 3 lines.
12         int answer =
13         AddTwoNumbers(number1, number2) +
14         AddTwoNumbers(number1, number3);
15
16         DisplayResult(answer);
17     }
18
19     int AddTwoNumbers (int firstNumber, int secondNumber)
20     {
21         int result = firstNumber + secondNumber;
22         return result;
23     }
24
25     void DisplayResult(int total)
26     {
27         Debug.Log("The grand total is: " + total);
28     }
29
30 }
```

What just happened?

As you can see in the following screenshot, the result is **14**. However, the main concept to learn from this example is this:

- When a method returns a value, it's a type of data just like a variable would store
- In fact, the value returned from a method could easily be stored in a variable

Analysis of the code is as follows:

- The code on line 10 and its description is as follows:

```
void Start()
```

Unity calls the `Start()` method once only.

- The code on lines 12 to 14 and its description is as follows: (Note: I have put this single statement on three lines for a better screenshot.)

```
int answer =
AddTwoNumbers(number1, number2) +
AddTwoNumbers(number1, number3);
```

All this line does is add two numbers and store the result in a variable named "answer".

First there is a call to `AddTwoNumbers(number1, number2)` on line 19.

The arguments `number1` and `number2` send the integers 2 and 3 to the method parameters on line 19.

- The code on line 19 and its description is as follows:

```
int AddTwoNumbers(int firstNumber, int secondNumber);
```

The integers 2 and 3 are assigned to the parameter variables `firstNumber` and `secondNumber`.

- The code on line 21 and its description is as follows:

```
int result = firstNumber + secondNumber;
```

The numbers 2 and 3 are added and stored in the declared variable result.

◆ The code on line 22 and its description is as follows:

```
return result;
```

The integer 5, stored in the variable result, is returned back to line 12, where the method was called.

◆ Back to the code on line 12 with its description:

Where you see `AddTwoNumbers(number1, number2)`, now sits the integer 5. The substitution has taken place.

Now, line 12 continues its execution with another call to:
`AddTwoNumbers(number1, number3)` on line 19

The only difference is that the arguments have changed.

The arguments `number1` and `number3` send the integers 2 and 7 to the method parameters on line 19.

◆ Back to the code on line 19 again with its explanation:

The integers 2 and 7 are assigned to the parameter variables `firstNumber` and `secondNumber`.

◆ The code on line 21 and its description:

`2` and `7` are added and stored in result.

◆ The code on line 22 with its description:

The integer 9, stored in result, is returned back to line 12, where the method was called.

◆ Back to the code on line 12 again with its description:

Where you see `AddTwoNumbers(number1, number3)`, now sits the integer `9`. The substitution has taken place.

Now line 12 continues its execution. There is a plus sign between the two method calls which means `5` and `9` are added together and the resultant integer `14` is now stored in the variable answer.

The `Start()` method code block now continues execution on line 16.

◆ The code on line 16 and its description is as follows:

```
DisplayResult(answer);
```

This is calling the `DisplayResult()` method on line 25.

It takes one argument. The argument used is the variable answer which stores a value of type `int`.

The argument answer sends the integer 14 to the method parameter on line 25.

- The code on line 25 with its descripton:

  ```
  void DisplayResult(int total)
  ```

  The integer 14 is assigned to the parameter variable total.

- The code on line 27 and its description:

  ```
  Debug.Log("The grand total is: " + total);
  ```

  This output to the Unity **Console** includes a little peek into the next chapter.

  Some text is displayed as well as the value stored in the variable total.

  The Unity **Console** displays **The grand total is: 14**.

  The Start() method is done executing its code. Since there is no further code in LearningScript to execute, the script is done.

Have a go hero – add two more numbers together

Try modifying line 12 to add the numbers together that are stored in the variables number2 and number3. You will have to include an additional call to AddTwoNumbers(). The result in the **Console** should be **The grand total is: 24**.

Calling a method is a logic detour

As you can see by following the code analysis, code is executed one step at a time. However, calling a method does send code execution on a detour. The method is then executed one line at a time until the end of the method is reached. If the method return type is void, then execution restarts from the point where the method was called. If the method returns a value, then the value returned is substituted at the place the method was called, then execution restarts from the point of substitution.

Using Unity's Update and Start methods

Every time you create a script in Unity, these two skeleton methods are included. That's because they are rather important. These are the most commonly used MonoBehaviour methods, see the next screenshot for others. I like to call these Unity's magic methods because you don't call these methods, Unity does. It's usually important that at least one MonoBehaviour method is included in a Unity script to cause the script to execute. I say usually because other methods in the script may be called from another script or class.

How do I know these two methods are called by Unity and that they are MonoBehaviour methods? Here, the Unity **Scripting Reference** is your friend.

Here's just a portion of the methods Unity can call in a script. This is from the **Scripting Reference**. Just search for `MonoBehavior`:

Overridable Functions
Update
LateUpdate
FixedUpdate
Awake
Start

Look at line 4 of **LearningScript**:

```
public class LearningScript : MonoBehaviour
```

This line says that `LearningScript` inherits from `MonoBehaviour`. Any script that inherits from `MonoBehaviour` will automatically call the methods `Update()` and `Start()` if they are in the script. Therefore, if you want, you can create a script in MonoDevelop instead of Unity, just have it inherit from `MonoBehavior` by adding: `: MonoBehaviour` after the class name.

 Please notice the **colon** that needs to be included.

The Start method is called one time

Unity calls this method only one time. When the GameObject your script is attached to is first used in your scene, the `Start()` method is called. This method is primarily used to initialize, or setup, the member variables in your script. This allows everything in your script to be ready to go before `Update()` is called for the first time.

You've probably noticed that many of the examples I used in `LearningScript` are making use of `Start()`. These examples weren't initializing any code, I was just taking advantage of the fact that since `Start()` is only called once, displaying output to the Console would, therefore, only be displayed once, which just made it easier to see the output displayed.

The Update method is called over and over and over...

As you study the sample code in the **Scripting Reference**, you will notice that a vast majority of the code is in the `Update()` method. As your game runs, the Scene is displayed many times per second. This is called **Frames per Second**, or **FPS**. After each frame is displayed, the `Update()` method is called by Unity to run your code.

Since `Update()` is called every frame, it allows your game to detect input, such as mouse clicks and key presses, every frame. User input is one of the topics we are about to cover in the next chapter.

Pop quiz – understanding method operation

Q1. What are the minimum requirements for defining a method?

Q2. What is the purpose of the parentheses at the end of the method's name?

Q3. What does void mean in a method definition?

Q4. In a Unity script, how is the `Update()` called?

Summary

In this chapter, we learned that a method definition ends with a code block between two curly braces, not with a semicolon. The parentheses are part of a method's name. We also learned how to call a method into action, how to use data returned from a method, and that Unity calls some methods automatically, such as the `Start()` and `Update()` methods, when the script inherits from the `MonoBehaviour` class.

You now know the two major building blocks of scripting, variables and methods. From now on, everything else you do will just be making use of variables and methods. Now that you understand these two building blocks, you are ready for the next chapter that deals with making decisions in your code.

5
Making Decisions in Code

One of the primary duties of a computer is controlling what happens next when certain conditions are met. That's what computers do whether the code is controlling an application or a game. We write scripts to make GameObjects behave a certain way one moment, then the behavior should change when the conditions change. A script has to detect when the conditions change, then make the appropriate code execute based on the new conditions. This chapter looks at some examples of the ways that conditions can change, and the code to detect these changes. This in turn determines which code in the script is executed next.

In this chapter we will discuss:

- ◆ If statement decisions
- ◆ Checking for many conditions
- ◆ If-else statement decisions
- ◆ User's input condition changes
- ◆ Looping though data in an Array, List, or Dictionary

Let's begin...

Testing conditions with an if statement

If, if, if. If I do this... if I do that... What happens if...

Certainly you've had to make decisions about all kinds of things in your life every day. We all do it all the time without actually giving the process of making a decision much thought, if any. As we make daily decisions, most of the time we just do the decision processing in our head. Unity doesn't have that human luxury, so we have to write it out so Unity can know the conditions that lead to certain choices. Having to write the logic is the strange part of writing code for beginners, simply because people usually make the vast majority of decision without writing anything down first. However, it is very simple to do.

An `if` statement is the most common way GameObjects make decisions. Data used to make these decisions is the information usually stored in some variables. For an if statement it's as easy as saying "If my condition is met, then execute my code block."

Testing if conditions are true or false

A sampling of conditions that can be true or false:

- The user pressed a button
- The temperature is cold
- The character died
- The bear made big potty in the woods

General questions like these are answered by humans, usually, with either a yes or no. For Unity, the answers will be either true or false. For example: "the bear made big potty in the woods" is either true, or false.

Time for action – create a couple of if statements

The **if** statements work by determining whether a condition inside a pair of parentheses is true or false.

1. Modify `LearningScript` as shown in the next screenshot.
2. Save the file.
3. In Unity, click on Play.

```
 1 ⊟ using UnityEngine;
 2 ⌐ using System.Collections;
 3
 4 ⊟ public class LearningScript : MonoBehaviour
 5   {
 6 ⊟     void Start ()
 7       {
 8           bool theBearMadeBigPottyInTheWoods = true;
 9
10 ➤       if(theBearMadeBigPottyInTheWoods)
11         {
12             Debug.Log("This is true, and it's stinky, too.");
13         }
14
15           theBearMadeBigPottyInTheWoods = false;
16
17 ➤       if((!)theBearMadeBigPottyInTheWoods)
18         {
19             Debug.Log("Of course NOT, it's a polar bear.");
20         }
21       }
22   }
```

What just happened?

Here's the output in the Unity **Console**:

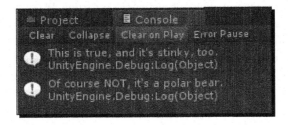

Code analysis:

- The code on line 8 is as follows:

  ```
  bool theBearMadeBigPottyInTheWoods = true;
  ```

  This Boolean variable is declared and assigned the value of `true`.

- The code on line 10 and its description:

  ```
  if( theBearMadeBigPottyInTheWoods)
  ```

  An `if` statement to test if the condition between the parenthesis is `true` or `false`.

  The variable `theBearMadeBigPottyInTheWoods` is storing a value `true`, therefore.The code block on lines 11 to 13 is executed, as shown in the **Console** screenshot.

Using the NOT operator to change the condition

Here's a little curveball to wrap your mind around, the NOT logical operator. It's written in code using an exclamation mark. This makes a true condition false, or a false condition true.

- The code on line 15 along with its description:

  ```
  theBearMadeBigPottyInTheWoods = false;
  ```

  Assigns the value `false` to `theBearMadeBigPottyInTheWoods`.

- The code on line 17 with its description is as follows:

  ```
  if( ! theBearMadeBigPottyInTheWoods)
  ```

  Another if statement, but this time `theBearMadeBigPottyInTheWoods` is false.

  However, there's a NOT logical operator in front of the variable. See the exclamation mark in the red circle shown in the previous screenshot.

  This means the if statement condition is NOT false, which is the same as saying true. Therefore the code block on lines 18 to 20 will be executed, as shown in the Console screenshot

  The code block on lines 18 to 20 will be executed, as shown in the Console screenshot

I can already hear your question, why not just check for true? As you will discover when writing if statements, you need to be able to make decisions based on whether a condition is true, or if the condition is false. You want the option to execute a code block for either of these two conditions. For example, you may want to execute some code based on whether a user didn't press a button at a particular time. If the user did not press the button, then execute the code block.

Checking many conditions in an if statement

Sometimes you will want your if statements to check many conditions before any code block is executed. This is very easy to do. There are two more logical operators that you can use:

- AND: It is used by putting && between the conditions being checked.
- OR: It is used by putting || between the conditions being checked.

Time for action – create if statements with more than one condition to check

1. Modify `LearningScript` as shown in the next screenshot.
2. Save the file.
3. In Unity, click on Play.

```
1   using UnityEngine;
2   using System.Collections;
3
4   public class LearningScript : MonoBehaviour
5   {
6       void Start ()
7       {
8           bool theBearMadeBigPottyInTheWoods = true;
9           int temperature = 40;
10
11          if(temperature >= 35 && theBearMadeBigPottyInTheWoods)
12          {
13              Debug.Log("Both conditions are true.");
14          }
15
16          if(temperature >= 35 || theBearMadeBigPottyInTheWoods)
17          {
18              Debug.Log("Only takes one of these conditions to be true.");
19          }
20      }
21  }
```

 Notice line 11 is using the AND operator, and line 16 is using the OR operator.

What just happened?

Here is the output you get in the Unity **Console**:

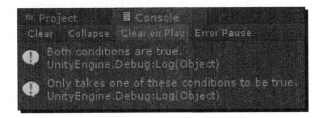

Code analysis:

♦ The code on line 8 and its description:

```
bool theBearMadeBigPottyInTheWoods = true;
```

A `bool` variable is declared and assigned the value of `true`.

♦ The code on line 9 with its description:

```
int temperature = 40;
```

An `int` variable is declared and assigned the value `40`.

- The code on line 11 with its description:

```
if(temperature >= 35 &&  theBearMadeBigPottyInTheWoods)
```

An `if` statement to test if both conditions are `true`.

The first test is checking if the `temperature` is greater then, or equal to, `35`.

The value stored in `temperature` is `40`, so this condition is true.

The value stored in `theBearMadeBigPottyInTheWoods` is true. Therefore the first condition and the second condition are true, so the code block executes.

- The code on line 16 with its description:

```
if(temperature >= 35 || theBearMadeBigPottyInTheWoods)
```

An `if` statement to test if either of the conditions are true.

We already know that both the conditions are true, and either the first condition or the second condition needs to be true. Therefore the code block will execute.

Have a go hero – change the value assigned to temperature

Try changing `temperature` to a lower value such as `30`. Only one of the `if` statements will be true:

The following is the analysis of code:

- The code on line 11 and its description is as follows:

```
if(temperature >= 35 && theBearMadeBigPottyInTheWoods)
```

Only one of the conditions is now true, as 30 is not greater then, or equal to, 35.

Therefore the first condition is false. Since both conditions have to be true, the code block does not execute.

- The code on line 16 and its description:

```
if(temperature >= 35 || theBearMadeBigPottyInTheWoods)
```

Only one of the conditions is now true.

30 is not greater then or equal to 35, therefore the first condition is false.

The second condition is true.

Since only one of the two conditions has to be true, doesn't make any difference which one, the code block executes.

Have a go hero – change theBearMadeBigPottyInTheWoods to false

Now change `theBearMadeBigPottyInTheWoods` to false as well. Now you see that neither of the if statements will execute their code blocks.

Using an if-else statement to execute alternate code

So far, the `if` statements have needed certain conditions to be `true` for the code block to execute. There is an option that allows you to have an alternate code block execute when the `if` statement conditions are `false`.

- If my conditions are met, execute the following code block, else execute the alternate code block

 This is very simple concept, just like a little kid saying: "If you give me an ice cream cone, I'll be nice, else I'm going to be naughty."

Time for action – add "else" to the if statement

if-else statements are just like regular **if statements** with the `else` option added.

1. Modify `LearningScript` as shown in the next screenshot.
2. Save the file.

3. In Unity, click on Play.

```
1  using UnityEngine;
2  using System.Collections;
3
4  public class LearningScript : MonoBehaviour
5  {
6      void Start ()
7      {
8          bool theBearMadeBigPottyInTheWoods = false;
9
10         if(theBearMadeBigPottyInTheWoods)
11         {
12             Debug.Log("This is executed because the condition is true");
13         }
14         else
15         {
16             Debug.Log("This is executed because the condition is false");
17         }
18     }
19 }
```

Line 14 shows how else, and its code block is simply added after the if code block.

What just happened?

The analysis of code is as follows:

♦ The code on line 8 and its description:

```
bool theBearMadeBigPottyInTheWoods = false;
```

The variable theBearMadeBigPottyInTheWoods is assigned the value of false.

♦ The code on line 10 and its description:

```
if( theBearMadeBigPottyInTheWoods)
```

Since the condition is false, the code block on lines 11 to 13 is not executed, and the script continues to line 14 of the if-else statement.

Therefore, the code block on lines 15 to 17 is executed instead:

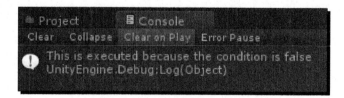

Pop quiz – understanding if statements

Q1. Humans can answer questions with a yes or no. What do C# if statements need as answers?

Q2. What logical operator can turn a `true` condition into `false`, or a `false` condition into `true`?

Q3. If two conditions have to be `true` to make an if statement's code execute, what logical operator would you use to join the conditions?

Q4. If only one of two conditions needed to be true to make an if statement's code execute, what logical operator would you use to join the two conditions?

Making decisions based on user input

Decisions always have to be made when the user provides input. In *Chapter 2, Introducing the Building Blocks for Unity Scripts,* we used an example where the user had to press the **Return/Enter** key to call the `AddTwoNumbers()` method:

```
if(Input.GetKeyUp(Keycode.Return))
AddTwoNumbers();
```

The `if` statement condition becomes true only when the `Return` key is released after being pressed down. Here's a partial screenshot of the `GetKeyUp()` method as shown in the **Scripting Reference**:

Input.**GetKeyUp**

static bool **GetKeyUp**(KeyCode **key**);

Description
Returns true during the frame the user releases the key identified by the key KeyCode enum parameter.

After the `Return` key is released, `AddTwoNumbers()` is executed.

 Notice that the code, `AddTwoNumbers()`, isn't between two curly braces. When there is only one line of code to execute for an if or an else, you have the option to not use the curly braces.

Storing data in an array, a List, or a Dictionary

There are times that many items need to be stored in some type of list. Perhaps a selection of weapons that a character may use. An example used later in this book is a list of splashscreens for the State Machine project we will build.

There are basically two ways to access items in a list:

◆ **Direct retrieval**: The location of an item in the list is already known, so code is written to access it directly, or

◆ **Loop retrieval**: The location of an item in the list is not known, it's just in there somewhere, so code is written to loop through the list until the item desired is found.

First though, we need a list of items before we can select anything from the list. An example of collecting items into a list, then looping through the list, is shown in the **Scripting Reference** under the `GetComponents()` method:

```
public HingeJoint[] hingeJoints;
void Example() {
  hingeJoints = gameObject.GetComponents<HingeJoint>();
  ...
  }
```

All the `HingeJoints` in a GameObject are collected into an array (list). Once all the `HingeJoints` are in the array, it's up to us to decide which `HingeJoints` we want to work with in our code.

So bottom line, what are we talking about here? We know that a variable stores a single item. For instance, we could store a single weapon in a variable. That's great as long as we only have one weapon. Suppose we have the option of using many different weapons. To store these weapons we would need a separate variable for each one. A better option would be to store all the weapons in some sort of super-variable that can store many items, that way they're all stored in one place, not in a whole bunch of different variables.

That's what an array, a List, or a Dictionary is, a variable with the ability to store many items. Like a super-variable divided into many cubbyholes.

Storing items in an array

Looking at the `GetComponents()` example on the **Scripting Reference**, let's see how an array is created:

- As per the code on line 1: `public HingeJoint[] hingeJoints;`
    - `public` means this array will appear in the **Inspector**. Also the array is accessible from other scripts.
    - `HingeJoint[]` is the type of variable being created. It's going to be a `HingeJoint` type (`HingeJoint` is a class in the **Scripting Reference**).
    - The square brackets specify that the variable created is going to be an array, a variable with many cubby-holes to store several `HingeJoint` objects, and only `HingeJoint` objects.
    - `hingeJoint` is the name of the array being created.

That was easy enough. It's just like creating any other variable. The only difference was the addition of the square brackets to specify that the type of variable being declared is actually going to be an array.

Now that the array is created, the `GetComponent()` method retrieves all the `HingeJoints` on the GameObject and stores each of them into the array:

- As per the code on line 3: `hingeJoints = gameObject.` `GetComponents<HingeJoint>();`
    - `hingeJoints` is the array
    - GameObject is the variable that stores the GameObject this script is attached to
    - `GetComponents<HingeJoint>()` is the method used to find every `HingeJoint` object on this GameObject

As each `HingeJoint` object is found, it is stored into one of the cubbyholes of the array. These cubbyholes actually have a real name called an **element**. These elements actually have a specific location inside the `hingeJoint` array. Each element is given an index number. The first `HingeJoint` found would be stored in the element at index 0, the second one found is stored in the element at index 1. The third at index 2, and on and on until all the `HingeJoints` are found on the GameObject.

So if we knew exactly, which `HingeJoint` in the array we wanted to work with, perhaps the second `HingeJoint` which is stored in the element at index 1, we can simply retrieve it directly by saying it's stored in the variable:

```
hingeJoint[1]
```

Once again we use the square brackets because the variable is actually an array, and also to specify the index number.

Please notice that the very first index number starts with zero. This is called zero indexed. It's just something you will have to remember. Many things in programming are zero indexed, and it creates coding errors when you forget, especially for beginners.

That's all I want to say about using arrays to store objects because I want to discuss using a `List` instead. It's like an array with extra benefits.

Storing items in a List

Using a `List` instead of an array can be so much easier to work with in a script. Look at some forum sites related to C#, and Unity, and you'll discover that a great deal of programmers simply don't use an array unless they have to, they prefer to use a `List`.

Here are the basics of why a List is better, and easier, to use than an array:

- An array is a fixed size and unchangeable
- The size of a `List` is adjustable
- You can easily add to, and remove elements from a `List`
- To mimic adding a new element to an array, we would need to create a whole new array with the desired number of elements, then copy over the old elements

The first thing to understand is that a `List` has the ability to store any type of object, just like an array. Also, just like an array, we must specify, which type of object you want a particular `List` to store. This means that if you want a `List` of integers, of the `int` type, then you can create a `List` that will store only the `int` type. Want a `List` of pony names? Then create a `List` that will store only the `string` type.

Time for action – create a List of pony names

Create a `List` that stores the names of some ponies. Since they are names, use the `string` type.

1. Modify `LearningScript` as shown in the next screenshot.
2. Notice the change on line 2.
3. Save the file.

4. In Unity, click on Play.

```
1   using UnityEngine;
2   using System.Collections.Generic;
3
4   public class LearningScript : MonoBehaviour
5   {
6       void Start ()
7       {
8           List<string> myFavoritePonies = new List<string>();
9
10          myFavoritePonies.Add("Princess Cadence");
11          myFavoritePonies.Add("Fluttershy");
12          myFavoritePonies.Add("Nightmare Moon");
13
14          Debug.Log("This List has " + myFavoritePonies.Count + " ponies.");
15
16          Debug.Log("The pony's name at index 1 is " + myFavoritePonies[1]);
17          Debug.Log("The pony's name at index 2 is " + myFavoritePonies[2]);
18          Debug.Log("The pony's name at index 0 is " + myFavoritePonies[0]);
19      }
20  }
```

What just happened?

The following screenshot is the **Console** output. Notice the first output tells you there is a total of 3 elements in the `List`:

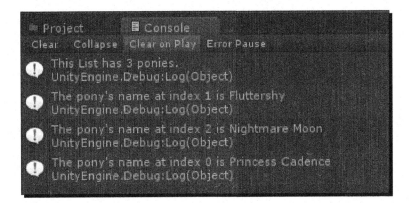

Please notice that your code is using dot syntax, which will be discussed in more detail in the next chapter. The main concepts I want you to focus on here are the features of a `List`.

The analysis of code is as follows:

- The code on line 2 is as follows:

```
Using System.Collections.Generic;
```

To be able to use a `List`, this tells Unity where to find the necessary C# code files for using a `List`.

Change the using statement to `using System.Collections.Generic;`.

- The code on line 8 is as fololws:

```
List<string> myFavoritePonies = new List<string>();
```

This statement creates an empty `List` object.

First thing to notice is that `List<string>` specifies that you are creating a `List` of type `string`.

The name of the `List` is `myFavoritePonies`.

Everything on the left side of the assignment operator (=) is creating a variable, declaring the type and the name.

Everything on the right side is just like assigning a value to a variable, therefore `new List<string()` is a method called to create a new `List` object in computer memory, and give that memory location the name of `myFavoritePonies`.

What is different here is that `List` is an object that itself can store data in elements. Imagine an egg carton as an object that can store the egg type. Creating objects will be discussed more in the next chapter about dot syntax.

♦ The code between lines 10 to 12:

```
myFavoritePonies.Add("Princess Cadence");
```

These three lines of code are adding `strings`, the pony names, to the `myFavoritePonies` List.

Just like an array, each pony name `string` added is given an index number for the element that each pony name is stored in:

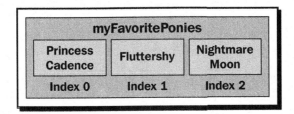

♦ The code on line 14 is as follows:

```
Debug.Log("This List has " + myFavoritePonies.Count + " ponies");
```

`myFavoritePonies.Count` retrieves the number of elements in the `List`.

♦ The code between lines 16 and 18:

```
Debug.Log("The pony's name at index 1 is " + myFavoritePonies[1]);
```

Here you see the index number inside square brackets. Just like an array, this is how to directly retrieve the data in an element at a specific index.

Like the array, the first element in a `List` is at index 0.

Have a go hero – add another pony to the List

Add another pony to the `List`, then display it's name. Also, in the **Console**, display the number of elements in the `List` after adding the fourth pony.

```
using UnityEngine;
using System.Collections.Generic;

public class LearningScript : MonoBehaviour
{
    void Start ()
    {
        List<string> myFavoritePonies = new List<string>();

        myFavoritePonies.Add("Princess Cadence");
        myFavoritePonies.Add("Fluttershy");
        myFavoritePonies.Add("Nightmare Moon");

        Debug.Log("This List has " + myFavoritePonies.Count + " ponies.");

        Debug.Log("The pony's name at index 1 is " + myFavoritePonies[1]);
        Debug.Log("The pony's name at index 2 is " + myFavoritePonies[2]);
        Debug.Log("The pony's name at index 0 is " + myFavoritePonies[0]);

        myFavoritePonies.Add("Rainbow Dash");

        Debug.Log("The pony's name at index 3 is " + myFavoritePonies[3]);

        Debug.Log("This List now has " + myFavoritePonies.Count + " ponies.");
    }
}
```

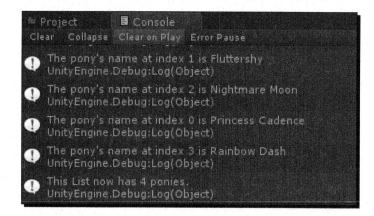

 Adding an element to the `List` shows the flexibility it has over an array. This is impossible to do using an array.

Storing items in a Dictionary

A dictionary has a Key/Value pair. The **Key** is just like an index in an array or list, it's associated with a particular value. The big benefit of a dictionary is that we can specify what the key is going to be. We have to specify the type and the name of the key that will be associated with the value stored.

A real world example you're familiar with is a collection of customers and their ID number. Just by knowing the customer's ID, you could retrieve the customer's information.

Time for action – create a dictionary of pony names and keys

Create a `Dictionary` using type `int` for the keys.

1. Modify `LearningScript` as shown in the next screenshot.
2. Save the file.
3. In Unity, click on Play.

```
 1  using UnityEngine;
 2  using System.Collections.Generic;
 3
 4  public class LearningScript : MonoBehaviour
 5  {
 6      void Start ()
 7      {
 8          Dictionary<int,string> myFavoritePonies = new Dictionary<int,string>();
 9
10          myFavoritePonies.Add(10, "Princess Cadence");    2 ways to add to a Dictionary
11          myFavoritePonies.Add(20, "Fluttershy");
12          myFavoritePonies[30] = "Nightmare Moon";
13
14          Debug.Log("The pony's name for Key 10 is " + myFavoritePonies[10]);
15          Debug.Log("The pony's name for Key 20 is " + myFavoritePonies[20]);
16          Debug.Log("The pony's name for Key 30 is " + myFavoritePonies[30]);
17
18          myFavoritePonies[40] = "Rainbow Dash";
19
20          Debug.Log("The pony's name for Key 40 is " + myFavoritePonies[40]);
21
22          Debug.Log("This Dictionary has " + myFavoritePonies.Count + " ponies.");
23      }
24  }
```

What just happened?

Here is the output to Unity's **Console**.

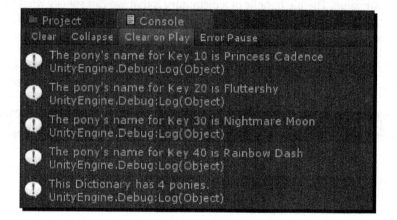

The analysis of code is as follows:

- The code on line 8 is as follows:

  ```
  Dictionary<int, string> myFavoritePonies = new Dictionary<int,
      string>();
  ```

  Declaring a `Dictionary` is very similar to declaring a `List`.

  A `Dictionary` requires you to specify the type for the `Key`.

  This example used integers for the keys.

- The code on lines 10 and 11 is as follows:

  ```
  myFavoritePonies.Add(10, "Princess Cadence");
  myFavoritePonies.Add(20, "Fluttershy");
  ```

  Here you added two ponies using `Add`, just like you did for a `List`.

- The code on lines 12 and 18 with its description is as follows:

  ```
  myFavoritePonies[30] = "Nightmare Moon";
  myFavoritePonies[40] = "Rainbow Dash";
  ```

  Here you added ponies by assigning the pony name to a particular dictionary key.

Using a Collection Initializer to add items to a List or Dictionary

There is another way to add elements to a List or Dictionary. So far you have declared and created a new empty List and Dictionary, then added ponies to them on separate lines of code. You can add the ponies at the same time you declare the List or Dictionary with a Collection Initializer.

Time for action – adding ponies using a Collection Initializer

If we know the items to add ahead of time, we can add them when we create the List or Dictionary.

1. Modify LearningScript as shown in the next screenshot.
2. Save the file.
3. In Unity, click on Play.

```
1   using UnityEngine;
2   using System.Collections.Generic;
3
4   public class LearningScript : MonoBehaviour
5   {
6       void Start ()
7       {
8           List<string> myFavoritePonies = new List<string>()
9               {"Princes Cadence", "Fluttershy"};
10
11          Debug.Log("The pony's name at index 0 is " + myFavoritePonies[0]);
12          Debug.Log("The pony's name at index 1 is " + myFavoritePonies[1]);
13
14          Dictionary<int, string> ponyDictionary = new Dictionary<int, string>()
15              {{10,"Nightmare Moon"},{20,"Rainbow Dash"}};
16
17          Debug.Log("The pony's name at Key 10 is " + ponyDictionary[10]);
18          Debug.Log("The pony's name at Key 20 is " + ponyDictionary[20]);
19      }
20  }
```

What just happened?

Here's the **Console** output:

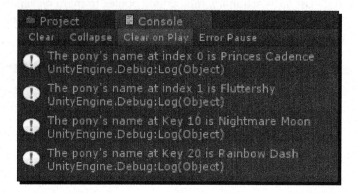

The analysis of the code is as follows:

- The code on lines 8 and 9 with its description:

```
List<string> myFavoritePonies = new List<string>() {"Princess
   Cadence", Fluttershy"};
```

This is actually a single statement. It's on two lines to make it fit the screenshot.

Line 9 shows the **Collection Initializer** that's been added to the usual `List` declaration.

Notice the pony names are between two curly braces. This is not a code block. This is another use of curly braces.

This `List` Collection Initializer is the two curly braces and the strings, the pony names, that are between them.

Notice there is a semicolon after the last curly brace. This ends the `List` declaration statement.

- The code between lines 14 and 15:

```
Dictionary<int, string> ponyDictionary = new Dictionary<int,
   string>() {{10, "Nightmare Moon"}, {20, "Rainbow Dash"}};
```

This is a single statement. It's on two lines to make it fit the screenshot.

Line 15 shows the **Collection Initializer** that's been added to the usual `Dictionary` declaration.

Each key and value pony name is between two curly braces, then all the key/value pair combinations being initialized are between two curly braces.

Pop quiz – understanding an array and a List

Q1. In an array or a List, what is an element?

Q2. In an array or a List, what is the index number of the first element?

Q3. Can a single array, or a single List, store different types of data?

Q4. How can you add more elements to an array to make room for more data?

Looping though lists to make decisions

These previous array, List, and Dictionary examples showed how to get data into them, and how they store data. It's now time to learn how to loop through the data to retrieve the needed data.

Here are some common ways to perform loops:

- ◆ `foreach` loop
- ◆ `for` loop
- ◆ `while` loop

Using the foreach loop

When working with Collections such as an array, a list or dictionary, the preferred way to cycle through the elements and retrieve data is to use the `foreach` loop.

Time for action – using foreach loops to retrieve data

We're going to create an array, a list and a dictionary, then loop through each one to retrieve the desired data from each one by using `foreach` loops.

1. Modify `LearningScript` as shown in the next screenshot.
2. Save the file.

3. In Unity, click on Play.

```
1  using UnityEngine;
2  using System.Collections.Generic;
3
4  public class LearningScript : MonoBehaviour
5  {
6
7      void Start ()
8      {
9          string[] ponyArray = new string[]
10             {"AppleJack", "Rarity"};
11
12         foreach(string pony in ponyArray)
13         {
14             if(pony == "Rarity")
15                 Debug.Log("I was looking for " + pony);
16         }
17
18         List<string> ponyList = new List<string>()
19             {"Princess Cadence", "Fluttershy"};
20
21         foreach(string pony in ponyList)
22         {
23             if(pony == "Fluttershy")
24                 Debug.Log("I was looking for " + pony);
25         }
26
27         Dictionary<int, string> ponyDictionary = new Dictionary<int, string>()
28             {{10, "Nightmare Moon"}, {20, "Rainbow Dash"}};
29
30         foreach(KeyValuePair<int, string> pony in ponyDictionary)
31         {
32             if(pony.Key == 20)
33                 Debug.Log("I was looking for " + pony.Value);
34         }
35     }
36 }
```

What just happened?

As we looped through each list, we decided which data to display to the **Console**:

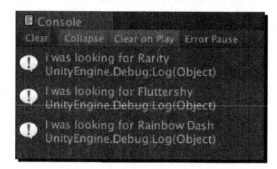

The analysis of the code is as follows:

For each list we created, we populated them using a Collection Initializer.

- The code between lines 9 and 10 with its description:

```
string[] ponyArray = new string[] {"AppleJack", "Rarity"};
```

A `string` array named `ponyArray` is declared and two strings are added.

- The code on line 12 with its description is as follows:

```
foreach(string pony in ponyArray)
```

A `foreach` loop is used to retrieve one element, a pony name string, stored in `ponyArray`.

A variable is declared named `pony` to hold the retrieved pony name.

Once a pony name is retrieved, the `foreach` code block, lines 13 to 16, is executed.

This looping continues until each element in `ponyArray` has been retrieved and tested in the code block.

- The code on line 14 with its description is as follows:

```
if(pony == "Rarity");
```

If the retrieved string stored in `pony` is equal to `"Rarity"`, then line 15 executes.

- The code on line 15 with its description is as follows:

```
Debug.Log("I was looking for " + pony);
```

The string I was looking for plus the string value stored in pony is displayed in the **Console**.

- The code between lines 18 and 19 with its description:

```
List<string> ponyList = new List<string>() {"Princess Cadence",
    "Fluttershy"};
```

A `List` named `ponyList` is declared that will store the `string` type, and two strings are added.

- The code on line 21 with its description is as follows:

```
foreach(string pony in ponyList)
```

A `foreach` loop is used to retrieve one element, a pony name `string`, stored in `ponyList`.

A variable is declared named `pony` to hold the retrieved pony name.

Once a pony name is retrieved, the `foreach` code block (that is, lines 22 to 25) is executed.

This looping continues until each element in `ponyList` has been retrieved and tested in the code block.

◆ The code on line 23 with its description is as follows:

```
if(pony == "Fluttershy")
```

If the retrieved string stored in `pony` is equal to `"Fluttershy"`, then line 24 executes.

◆ The code on line 24 with its description is as follows:

```
Debug.Log("I was looking for " + pony);
```

The string I was looking for plus the string value stored in `pony` is displayed in the **Console**.

◆ The code between lines 27 and 28 with its description:

```
Dictionary<int, string> ponyDictionary = new Dictionary<int,
    string>() {{10, "Nightmare Moon"}, {20, "Rainbow Dash"}};
```

A `Dictionary` named `ponyDictionary` is declared with key and value of type `<int, string>`, and two key/value pairs are added.

◆ The code on line 30 with its description is as follows:

```
foreach(KeyValuePair<int, string> pony in ponyDictionary)
```

A `foreach` loop is used to retrieve one `KeyValuePair`, a key and value, stored in `ponyDictionary`.

A variable is declared named `pony` to hold the retrieved `KeyValuePair`.

Once a key value and a pony name string are retrieved, the `foreach` code block (that is, lines 31 to 34) is executed.

This looping continues until each `KeyValuePair` in `ponyDictionary` has been retrieved and tested in the code block.

◆ The code on lines32 with its description is as follows:

```
if(pony.Key == 20)
```

If the retrieved `Key` stored in pony is equal to `20`, then line 33 executes.

◆ The code on line 33 with its description is as follows:

```
Debug.Log("I was looking for " + pony.Value);
```

The string I was looking for plus the string value stored in `pony.Key` is displayed in the **Console**.

Using the for loop

The best description I've found for a `for` loop: "Allows a code block to be executed a specific number of times."

The syntax of a `for` loop:

```
for (initializer; condition; iterator)
  {
    code block
  }
```

 Notice the three parts inside the parentheses are separated by semicolons, not commas.

Time for action – selecting a pony from a List using a for loop

Let's add four pony names to a `List`. Retrieve and display the number of elements in the `List`. Then use a `for` loop to display each pony name, and select one of them:

1. Modify `LearningScript` as shown in the next screenshot.

2. Save the file.

3. In Unity, click on Play.

```
1  using UnityEngine;
2  using System.Collections.Generic;
3
4  public class LearningScript : MonoBehaviour
5  {
6      void Start ()
7      {
8          List<string> ponyList = new List<string>()
9              {"Princess Cadence", "Fluttershy", "Rainbow Dash", "Rarity"};
10
11         Debug.Log("Number of elements in ponyList: " + ponyList.Count);
12
13         for(int i = 0; i < ponyList.Count; i++)
14         {
15             Debug.Log(ponyList[i]);
16
17             if(ponyList[i] == "Fluttershy")
18                 Debug.Log("I was looking for " + ponyList[i]);
19         }
20      }
21  }
```

What just happened?

The following screenshot shows the number of elements in `ponyList`, the names of the ponies we added to `ponyList`, and the pony we were looking for:

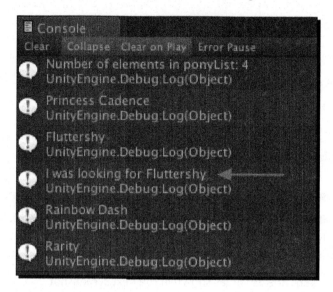

The analysis of the code is as follows:

◆ The code between lines 8 and 9 with its description:

```
List<string> ponyList = new List<string>() {"Princess
    Cadence", "Fluttershy", "Rainbow Dash", "Rarity"};
```

A `List` named `ponyList` is declared that will store the `string` type.

Four strings are added of the pony names.

◆ The code on line 11 with its description is as follows:

```
Debug.Log("Number of elements in ponyList: " + ponyList.Count);
```

The string `Number of elements in ponyList:` plus the number of elements used in `ponyList` is displayed in the **Console**.

`ponyList.Count` is using dot syntax to access the `Count` property, a variable that stores the number of elements in a `List`.

Four names were added to `ponyList`, so it has four elements to store the string names.

- The code on line 13 with its description is as follows:

```
for(int i = 0; i < ponyList.Count; i++)
```

The `for loop` is created.

The initializer is simply a declared variable that's assigned a value.

We declared a variable `i` of type `int`, and assigned it the a value of `0`. Why?

The first index number in a `List` is `0`.

The condition is checked for true before the code block, lines 14 to 19, is allowed to be executed.

When our `for` loop first begins, the variable `i` is equal to `0`, and `ponyList.Count` is equal to `4`, therefore `0` is less than `4`, which is `true`. Therefore the `for` loop code block is allowed to execute.

The iterator, `i++`, now adds 1 to `i`, making `i` now equal to 1.

`i++` is the same thing as writing `i = i + 1`, which means that you are taking the value in `i` and adding 1, then assigning that to `i`.

The loop repeats until the condition becomes `false`.

After four times through the loop, `i` is now equal to 4, therefore the condition is now `false` because `i` is not less than `4`, so the loop is finished.

 The letter "i" is typically used as the variable name in a for loop. It's tradition. If you happen to have nested for loops, then the variable names used will be the letters j, k, l, and so on, as needed.

- The code on lines 15 with its description is as follows:

```
Debug.Log(ponyList[i]);
```

The elements in `ponyList` are being access using the index number.

As the `for` loop is executed for the first time, `i` is equal to `0`, therefore

`ponyList[i]` is actually `ponyList[0]`, the element at index 0.

The element at index 0 is storing `Princess Cadence`.

After each iteration through the `for` loop, 1 is added to `i`, therefore the next trip through the for loop, `i` will be 1.

`ponyList[i]` will actually be `ponyList[1]`, the next element at index 1.

The result is all four ponies will be accessed and displayed in the **Console**.

◆ The code on lines 17 with its description is as follows:

```
if(ponyList[i] == "Fluttershy")
```

During each iteration through the code block, this if statement is checking to see if the name retrieved from `ponyList` is equal to `"Fluttershy"`.

When it is, line 18 is executed.

◆ The code on lines 18 with its description is as follows:

```
Debug.Log("I was looking for " + ponyList[i]);
```

The string `I was looking for` plus the name `Fluttershy` is displayed in the **Console**.

Using the while loop

The `while` loop executes a code block until a specified expression evaluates to false.

A `while` loop is very similar to a for loop. It's like breaking the `for` loop into component parts:

```
The syntax of a while loop:
initializer
while (condition)
{
  code block
  iterator
}
```

Time for action – finding data and breakout of the while loop

We're going to do something a little different in this loop. Once we find the pony we want, we'll breakout of the while loop. This is handy when looping through a large list of objects. When the desired data is found, there's no sense in continuing to loop through the rest of the list:

1. Modify `LearningScript` as shown in the next screenshot.

2. Save the file.

3. In Unity, click on Play.

```
1  using UnityEngine;
2  using System.Collections.Generic;
3
4  public class LearningScript : MonoBehaviour
5  {
6      void Start ()
7      {
8          List<string> ponyList = new List<string>()
9              {"Princess Cadence", "Fluttershy", "Rainbow Dash", "Rarity"};
10
11         int i = 0;
12         while(i < ponyList.Count)
13         {
14             Debug.Log(ponyList[i]);
15
16             if(ponyList[i] == "Rainbow Dash")
17             {
18                 Debug.Log("Stop. I was looking for " + ponyList[i]);
19                 break;
20             }
21             i++;
22         }
23     }
24 }
```

What just happened?

If we have been searching for Fluttershy instead of Rainbow Dash, and not included the break keyword on line 19, the output would have been exactly the same as the for loop example. In fact, the break keyword could have also have been used to breakout of the for loop.

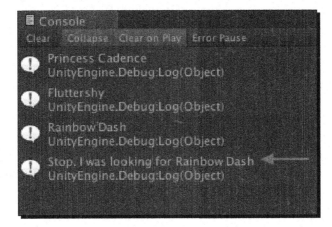

I will skip explaining lines of code that are identical in the `for` loop example.

The analysis of the code is as follows:

- The code on line 11 with its description is as follows:

```
int i = 0;
```

The initializer is declared and assigned the value of 1.

- The code on line 12 with its description is as follows:

```
while(i < ponyList.Count)
```

The `while` loop is declared with the condition.

Since `i` is 0, it is less than `ponyList.Count`, which is 4, the condition is true.

The `while` loop code block (that is, lines 13 to 22), is executed.

- The code on line 16 with its description is as follows:

```
if(ponyList[i] == "Rainbow Dash")
```

During each iteration through the code block, this `if` statement is checking to see if the name retrieved from `ponyList` is equal to `Rainbow Dash`.

When it is, the code block of lines 17 to 20 is executed.

When it isn't, line 21 is the next line that is executed.

- The code on line 21 with its description is as follows:

```
i++;
```

The iterator `i` is incremented by 1 and the loop repeats back to line 12 to check the condition again.

The loop repeats until `i` is equal to 4, making the condition false which exits the loop.

- The code on line 18 with its description is as follows:

```
Debug.Log("Stop. I was looking for " + ponyList[i]);
```

The string `Stop. I was looking for` plus the name `Rainbow Dash` is displayed in the **Console**.

- The code on line 19 with its description is as follows:

  ```
  break;
  ```

  `break` is a C# keyword that alters code flow.

  Code execution immediately leaves this `while` loop code block and continues to the first statement following the code block.

  There is no statement following the while loop, the script is finished.

Have a go hero – changing the pony name being searched

On line 16, change the pony name being searched and observe how it changes the number of pony names displayed in the **Console** before stopping.

Summary

There are unlimited ways to make decisions in code, however, we covered many of the common ways. The if statement is how the majority of decisions are made, including the if-else statements. Then we covered some of the sources that require making decisions, like user input, and using loops to evaluate data stored in arrays, lists and dictionaries. None of this is complicated. It's just a process of simple, logical steps.

Now that we've learned about the fundamentals of programming for writing scripts, it's time to dig into the world of objects. Since everything in Unity is an object, you need to know how to access the Components of an object, and how to communication between objects, by using dot syntax. You have seen some dot syntax used already in the examples we've coded. In next chapter, you will see how those dots work.

6

Using Dot Syntax for Object Communication

Scripts do many things by accessing the features built into Unity and third-party plugins. The Unity Scripting Reference is our link to the built-in Unity features. The thing is, exactly how do we invoke all of those Unity features?

So far all we've covered is basic C# programming. Granted, the example code we've seen has included some Dot Syntax, such as Debug.Log() to send output to Unity's Console. This is one of those Unity features. In the last chapter, we even saw some more Dot Syntax, pony.Key and pony.Value, which has nothing to do with Unity. These are just C# OOP (Object Oriented Programming) related features.

In both cases, there's some type of communication taking place to access methods and data to make things happen. To the beginner, those dots maybe odd looking and confusing, and they may ask, "What's the deal with all those darn dots between words?" Well, if you've been using the Internet and paid any attention at all, you've been using those dots, probably for years, and didn't pay much attention to them.

We see how to access the power of Dot Syntax as we cover the following sections:

- ◆ Dot Syntax being just an address
- ◆ Working with objects
- ◆ Using Dot Syntax in a script
- ◆ Accessing GameObjects using drag-and-drop versus writing code

So let's get on with it...

Using Dot Syntax is like addressing a letter

Ever seen something like this?

www.unity3d.com

That's right, a web address. Gee, I wonder why it's called a web **address**?

Simplifying the dots in Dot Syntax

Here is a fictitious mailing address:

Terry Norton

22 myStreet

Essex, VT

You've understood how to read an address like this since you were a kid. Let's take a look at it again using a different format:

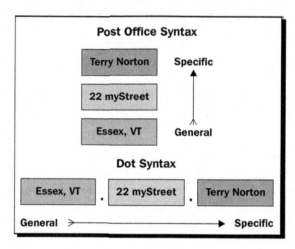

Looking at that, Dot Syntax isn't so confusing. It's just an address in a different format, in a way to locate things. Here's an example: imagine we met in Europe somewhere, and I ask you to get my sunglasses using only this information:

USA.Vermont.Essex.22 myStreet.2ndFloor.office.desk.center drawer.sunglasses

Would you have any problem locating them?

Using access modifiers for variables and methods

I could foresee one big issue trying to retrieve my sunglasses. My house isn't open to the public; it's a private residence, so the door is locked. This means you don't have access to the sunglasses.

The same rules of access apply to member variables and methods of a class or script.

In C#, when we create a member variable or method in a script, it is private by default. We can also explicitly specify that it's `private`.

Here, `private` means:

◆ A variable will not show in the **Inspector** as a Component property

◆ The variable or method will not be accessible from other scripts

We can specify a variable or method to be `public`.

Here, `public` means:

◆ A variable will show in the **Inspector** as a Component property

◆ The variable or method will be accessible from other scripts

Dot Syntax is the system used to locate and communicate with a variable or method in an object. To understand how to use Dot Syntax, we have to know the relationship between a class and its objects.

 A script always has access to its own member variable and methods whether they're `private` or `public`.

Working with objects is a class act

I'm throwing the word **object** around like you were born with the knowledge of what an object is. Actually you do know what it means. The coffee cup you may have in your hand is an object, a real one. That UFO flying around at night is an object; even if you can't identify it. In Unity, you may have a flying saucer in your Scene, but it's obviously not a real flying saucer, it's a virtual one. However, in the virtual world of gaming, most people would consider things they can see on the screen as objects.

If you can expand your mind just a little bit more, perhaps you can accept that not all objects in Unity have to be something you can see in a game Scene. In fact, the vast majority of objects in Unity are not visually in the Scene.

In a computer, an object is just a small section of your computer's memory that acts like a container. The container can have some data stored in variables and some methods to work with the data.

The best example I can show you is the object you've been using since you started this book.

In MonoDevelop, we've been working with the script called `LearningScript`. In Unity we use the general term **Script**, but it's actually a class, which means it's a definition of a type of container. Look at line 4 of the file:

```
public class LearningScript : MonoBehaviour
```

See that second word? That means that `LearningScript` is a class. In this class, we defined its member variables and methods. Any variable not declared in a method is a member variable of the class.

In *Chapter 2, Introducing the Building Blocks for Unity Scripts* I told you about the magic that happens when we attach the script (class) to a GameObject. Shazam!! The script becomes a Component object, a type of container for the GameObject that we defined as having some variables to store data and some methods to work that that data.

Besides the visual mesh in the Scene, can you visualize in your mind that a GameObject is just a bunch of different types of Component objects assembled together to construct that GameObject?

Each of those individual Components shown in the **Inspector** will become an object in our computer's memory when we click on the **Play** button.

Select any GameObject in the **Scene**, then look at the **Inspector**. For example, select the **Main Camera** GameObject. There are several Components on the **Main Camera** GameObject. Look at each of those defined Components. Every one of those Components started off as a class file in Unity, defining a type of container of variables and methods. We don't see or modify those Unity class files, but they're in Unity somewhere.

- The name of the class is also known as the object type of the object that will be created in memory from that class, when the **Play** button is clicked.

- Just like an `int`, or a `string` is a type of data, the name of a class is also a type of data.

- This means that when we declare a variable and specify the type of data it will store, it can just as easily store a reference to an object of the `LearningScript` type, as shown in the following line of code:

```
LearningScript myVariable;
```

- Storing a reference to an object in a variable does not mean we are storing the actual object. It means we are storing the location in memory of that object. It's just a reference that points to the object in memory so that the computer knows where to access the object's data and methods.This means we can have several variables storing a reference to the same object, but there's still only one actual object in memory.

A script is just a file on your hard drive, and there's only ever one file. The class file simply defines a type of container of variables and methods that will become a Component object in the memory when you click on **Play**. You can attach the script to many GameObjects, but there's still only one file on your hard drive.

Attaching a **Script** to a GameObject is like placing a sticky-note on the GameObject. When we click on the **Play** button, Unity looks at our GameObject, sees the sticky-note which says, "This GameObject is supposed to have a Component of type LearningScript. Make some room in the computer's memory to hold this object of variables and methods as described in the LearningScript class file."

If we were to attach LearningScript to 1000 GameObjects, and click on **Play**, there will be 1000 separate sections created in your computer's memory that each stores an object of type LearningScript. Each one has its own set of variables and methods, as described by the script file. Each one of those 1000 sections of computer memory is a separate Component object of its respective GameObject.

Even though the object created from a class is called a Component by Unity; in more general C# terms, each object that gets created from a class is called an instance object. A Component object and an instance object are the same thing.

Using Dot Syntax in a script

Now that you know that each Component object resides in computer memory, storing data in variables, it's time to use Dot Syntax to access those Component variables and methods.

Accessing a Component's own variables and methods

Dot Syntax can be used to access any pubic variable or method on any Component on any GameObject. Even though a Component always has access to its own variables and methods, we can still use Dot Syntax if we want.

In order to have access to a variable or method, we have to know its location. Let's start by looking in `LearningScript`.

Here's an overview of how to access a variable or method from within the current Component:

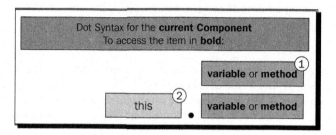

Time for action – accessing a variable in the current Component

Let's look at accessing a variable in `LearningScript` from inside `LearningScript`.

1. Modify `LearningScript` as shown in the following figure:

```
using UnityEngine;
using System.Collections.Generic;

public class LearningScript : MonoBehaviour
{
    string myString = "Access the variable ";

    void Start ()
    {
        Debug.Log("Press the Return key.");
    }

    void Update ()
    {
        if(Input.GetKeyDown(KeyCode.Return))
        {
            Debug.Log(myString + "the normal way.");
            Debug.Log(this.myString + "using 'this' keyword.");
            Debug.Log(GetComponent<LearningScript>().myString
                + "using GetComponent");

            Debug.Log(this);
            Debug.Log(GetComponent<LearningScript>());
        }
    }
}
```

this keyword

2. Save the file.

3. In Unity, click on **Play.**

What just happened?

Here are the outputs in the **Console**:

An analysis of the code shown in the previous code screenshot is as follows:

Line 6: `string myString = "Access the variable ";`

- ◆ `myString` is the variable that will be accessed
- ◆ Notice that it's `private` by default, yet it can still be accessed

Line 17: `Debug.Log(myString + "the normal way.");`

- ◆ This is how we have been accessing the value stored in a variable, by just using the variable name
- ◆ The `string` value in `myString`, `Accessing this variable`, is substituted for the variable name
- ◆ `myString` is being accessed without using Dot Syntax or `GetComponent()`, because a script always has access to its own variables and methods

Line 18: `Debug.Log(this.myString + "using 'this' keyword.");`

- ◆ `myString` is being accessed using Dot Syntax
- ◆ The `this` keyword refers to the current instance of the class, the current Component

Line 19: `Debug.Log(GetComponent<LearningScript>().myString + "using GetComponent.");`

- `myString` is being accessed using Dot Syntax again
- This time, the generic `GetComponent<T>()` method is retrieving the `LearningScript` Component

Line 22: `Debug.Log(this);`

- Using `this`, the Component is sent to the **Console** so we can see that `this` is the current `LearningScript` Component object

Line 23: `Debug.Log(GetComponent<LearningScript>());`

- Using `GetComponent<LearningScript>()`, the Component is sent to the **Console**, so we can see this also is the current `LearningScript` Component object
- The `this` keyword and `GetComponent<LearningScript>()` are both retrieving the same `LearningScript` Component object

Whoa!! What's with line 18?

Notice item 1 in the graphic under the section, *Accessing a Component's own variables and methods*? This is the usual way we will access variables and methods in the current script; no Dot Syntax required. This is how we've been doing it from the beginning of this book. It's how we will probably continue to access them. However, we do have the option of accessing the variables and methods in the current Component object using Dot Syntax.

As you can see from the output of lines 17 and 18, the value stored in `myString` is substituted no matter how we access `myString`.

So if we really wanted to, we could use the `GetComponent()` method to retrieve the current Component object of the `LearningScript` class in memory, then use Dot Syntax to access `myString`. However, C# provides a shortcut to get the current Component object by using the `this` keyword.

Item 2 in the graphic is the syntax used in line 18. In this example, the keyword `this` simply means the current instance object of the `LearningScript` class, the current Component.

> Why do I even mention using `this` at this time? Later on when we get into the State Machine, we will be using `this`. I want you to be aware of what `this` is, a substitute for the current instance object of a class.

Accessing another Component on the current GameObject

Now we start to just touch on the real power of Dot Syntax, communicating with other objects to access variable data and methods. We will now communicate with another Component on the same GameObject, the **Main Camera**. Remember, LearningScript is attached to the **Main Camera** already. The following diagram will explain how this is done:

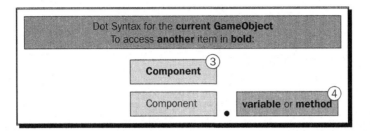

Time for action – communicating with another Component on the Main Camera

Let's create another script with a variable and a method, and attach it to the **Main Camera**, then have LearningScript communicate with it:

1. In Unity, create another **C# Script** and name it TalkToMe.

2. Make a public string variable named hereItIs.

3. Assign some text to hereItIs.

4. Make a public method named MakeMeTalk().

5. Have MakeMeTalk() output some text to the **Console**.

6. Attach MakeMeTalk() to the **Main Camera**. Now the code should look something like this:

```
1  using UnityEngine;
2  using System.Collections;
3
4  public class TalkToMe : MonoBehaviour
5  {
6      public string hereItIs = "This is the TalkToMe variable";
7
8      public void MakeMeTalk ()
9      {
10         Debug.Log("This is the TalkToMe method");
11     }
12 }
```

7. Modify `LearningScript` to retrieve the `TalkToMe` Component.

8. Modify `LearningScript` to retrieve the data in `hereItIs`.

9. Modify `LearningScript` to call the `MakeMeTalk()` method. Now the code snippet should look as follows:

```
1   using UnityEngine;
2   using System.Collections.Generic;
3
4   public class LearningScript : MonoBehaviour
5   {
6       TalkToMe otherComponent;
7
8       void Start ()
9       {
10          otherComponent = GetComponent<TalkToMe>();
11
12          Debug.Log("Press the Return key.");
13      }
14
15      void Update ()
16      {
17          if(Input.GetKeyDown(KeyCode.Return))
18          {
19              Debug.Log("This is the TalkToMe Component: " + otherComponent);
20              Debug.Log(otherComponent.hereItIs);
21              otherComponent.MakeMeTalk();
22          }
23      }
24  }
```

10. Save your scripts.

11. Click on **Play** in Unity.

What just happened?

Here's the output:

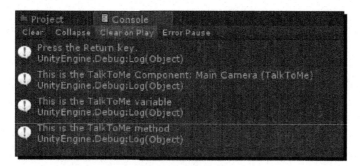

The `LearningScript` Component code retrieved a variable and called a method on the `TalkToMe` Component. Let's follow the code flow with these two Components.

An analysis of the code shown in the previous code screenshot is as follows:

On `LearningScript`:

Line 6: `TalkToMe otherComponent;`

- A variable `otherComponent` is declared to store a value of type `TalkToMe`
- A `TalkToMe` Component object will be created and stored in the variable `otherComponent`

Line 10: `otherComponent = GetComponent<TalkToMe>();`

- Remember, this is in the `Start()` method which Unity calls only once to initialize variables.
- The generic version of the `GetComponent<T>()` method is called to retrieve a reference to the `TalkToMe` Component object. This is item 3 on the previous graphic under the section, *Accessing another Component on the current GameObject*.
- The `<T>` part is the type of Component, the class name, that the method will return.
- This reference is stored in the variable `otherComponent`. Why? So that every time we need to use the `TalkToMe` Component with Dot Syntax, we can just use the reference stored in `otherComponent` instead of having to use `GetComponent<TalkToMe>()` each time.

Line 19: `Debug.Log("This is the TalkToMe Component: " + otherComponent);`

- This line of code sends the value stored in `otherComponent` to the Unity **Console** so we can see the reference that's pointing to the `TalkToMe` Component object

Line 20: `Debug.Log(otherComponent.hereItIs);`

- Dot Syntax is used to locate and retrieve the value stored in the variable `hereItIs` of the `TalkToMe` Component object. This is item 4 in the graphic under the section, *Accessing another Component on the current GameObject*.
- The `hereItIs` variable is declared on line 6 of the `TalkToMe` class.
- Notice that `hereItIs` is `public` so that it can be accessed from other scripts.
- If we didn't use `otherComponent`, we would have written the Dot Syntax expression like the following line of code:

  `GetComponent<TalkToMe>().hereItIs`

- The following is a screenshot of the **Scripting Reference** example:

At the time of this writing, Unity was updating its documentation. The page was not complete. The following screenshot is the old page; however, the code is still valid.

GameObject.GetComponent

function **GetComponent (type : Type) : Component**

Description
Returns the component of Type type if the game object has one attached, null if it doesn't. You can access both builtin components or scripts with this function.

GetComponent is the primary way of accessing other components. From javascript the type of a script is always the name of the script as seen in the project view. Example:

C# ▾

```
using UnityEngine;
using System.Collections;

public class example : MonoBehaviour {
    void Start() {
        Transform curTransform;
        curTransform = gameObject.GetComponent<Transform>();   ◄────
        curTransform = gameObject.transform;
    }
    void Update() {
        ScriptName other = gameObject.GetComponent<ScriptName>();   ◄────
        other.DoSomething();
        other.someVariable = 5;
    }
}
```

function **GetComponent.<T> () : T**   Click the link for more info

Description
Generic version. See the Generic Functions page for more details.

Line 21: `otherComponent.MakeMeTalk();`

- Dot Syntax is used to locate and call the `MakeMeTalk()` method of the `TalkToMe` Component object

- Code flow now jumps over to the `TalkToMe` class. This is also item 4 in the graphic under the section, *Accessing another Component on the current GameObject.*

On `TalkToMe`:

Line 8: `public void MakeMeTalk()`

- The `MakeMeTalk()` method is `public` so that it can be called from other scripts
- Its code block simply sends a string of text to the Unity **Console**
- The code block ends and code flow returns to the `LearningScript` class

On `LearningScript`:

Line 22: }

- Code flow has now reached the end of the `if` statement which began on line 17, and is waiting to detect if we press the *Return* key again

 Before you proceed further with the next section, remove the `TalkToMe` Component from the **Main Camera**. We are done with this script so there's no sense in having any of its Components hanging around.

Accessing other GameObjects and their Components

You just learned to access Components on the same GameObject. Now it's time to access other Gameobjects, and their Components using Dot Syntax.

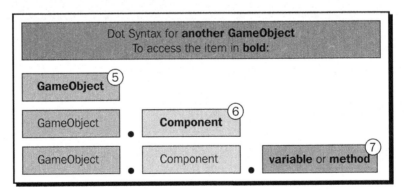

Time for action – creating two GameObjects and a new script

I want you to create one script that will be attached to two GameObjects. The script will have two methods that will cause the GameObjects to rotate left and right. This will show you that from a single script file, two separate Component objects will be created in the memory. Each Component object is a separate instance object with no absolutely knowledge of the other.

1. In your **Scene**, create two GameObjects, `Capsule` and `Cube`.

2. Add a **Directional Light** to the **Scene** so you can easily see the GameObjects.

3. Here's my **Scene** as an example:

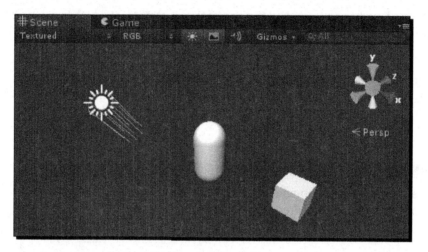

4. Create a new C# Script and name it Spinner.

5. Code the script as shown in the following screenshot:

```csharp
1  using UnityEngine;
2  using System.Collections;
3
4  public class Spinner : MonoBehaviour
5  {
6      public void SpinLeft()                    This means: 1 per second
7      {
8          transform.Rotate(0,0,60 * Time.deltaTime);
9      }
10                              x-axis  y-axis  z-axis
11     public void SpinRight()
12     {
13         transform.Rotate(0,0,-60 * Time.deltaTime);
14     }
15 }
```

6. Attach the `Spinner` script to the **Capsule** and the **Cube** GameObjects.

7. Modify `LeaningScript` as shown in the following screenshot:

```
1  using UnityEngine;
2  using System.Collections.Generic;
3
4  public class LearningScript : MonoBehaviour
5  {
6      GameObject capsuleGO;
7      Spinner cubeComp;
8
9      void Start ()
10     {
11         capsuleGO = GameObject.Find("Capsule");  ◄— ⑤
12         Debug.Log(capsuleGO);
13  ⑥ ► cubeComp = GameObject.Find("Cube").GetComponent<Spinner>();
14         Debug.Log(cubeComp);
15     }
16
17     void Update ()
18     {
19         if(Input.GetKey(KeyCode.LeftArrow))
20         {
21             capsuleGO.GetComponent<Spinner>().SpinLeft();  ◄— ⑦
22         }
23
24         if(Input.GetKey(KeyCode.RightArrow))
25         {
26             capsuleGO.GetComponent<Spinner>().SpinRight();◄— ⑦
27         }
28
29         if(Input.GetKey(KeyCode.UpArrow))
30         {
31             cubeComp.SpinLeft();
32         }
33
34         if(Input.GetKey(KeyCode.DownArrow))
35         {
36             cubeComp.SpinRight();
37         }
38     }
39 }
```

8. Save the file.

9. In Unity, click on **Play**.

What just happened?

Here's the output to the **Console**:

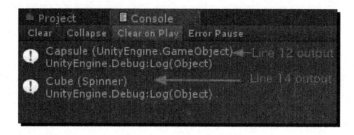

Now press the left and right arrow keys to make the Capsule spin, and the up and down arrow keys to make the Cube spin.

You created one script named `Spinner`, then attached the script to two separate GameObjects. When you click on **Play**, two separate `Spinner` Component objects are created in the computer memory. This is an example of how the `Spinner` class is just a blueprint, a description, of what each Component object created will be.

To access each `Spinner` Component from the `LearningScript` Component, you need to know about each GameObject that the `Spinner` Component is attached to.

This code is just a simple demonstration to show how Dot Syntax works. In real life, you may have each Component detect user input. On the other hand, perhaps you may want a class dedicated to processing user input. That's the neat thing about writing code, there are a zillion ways to accomplish a task.

An analysis of the code shown in the previous code screenshot is as follows:

On `LearningScript`:

Line 6: `GameObject capsuleGO;`

- A variable of type `GameObject` is declared
- The value this will store is a reference to the **Capsule** in the **Scene**

Line 7: `Spinner cubeComp;`

- A variable of type `Spinner` is declared
- The value this will store is a reference to a `Spinner` Component object created from the `Spinner` class

Line 9: `void Start()`

- The `Start()` method is used to allow the two variables to be initialized
- Remember, this method is called only once

Line 11: `capsuleGO = GameObject.Find("Capsule");`

- The `Find()` method of the `GameObject` class locates a GameObject in our **Scene**
- The reference to the **Capsule** GameObject is assigned to the variable `capsuleGO`
- This is item 5 in the previous graphic and also on the previous code screenshot

Line 12: `Debug.Log(capsuleGO);`

- This line was added just to show that the **Capsule** GameObject is in fact referenced in the variable `capsuleGO`

Line 13: `cubeComp = GameObject.Find("Cube").GetComponent<Spinner>();`

- This line shows how to retrieve a Component on a GameObject
- This retrieved reference to the `Spinner` Component object is on the **Cube** GameObject
- This is item 6 on the previous graphic and also on the previous code screenshot

Line 14: `Debug.Log(cubeComp);`

- This line was added just to show that the `Spinner` Component is part of the **Cube** GameObject, and is in fact referenced in the variable `cubeComp`

Line 19: `if(Input.GetKey(KeyCode.LeftArrow)`

- This `if` statement checks to see if the user has pressed the left arrow key
- If pressed, Line 21 of the code block is executed

Line 21: `capsuleGO.GetComponent<Spinner>().SpinLeft();`

- This line shows using Dot Syntax to locate a method in a Component of another GameObject.
- The `CapsuleGO` variable substitutes the reference to the **Capsule** GameObject
- The `Spinner` Component object is located on the **Capsule** GameObject
- The `SpinLeft()` method is called in the `Spinner` Component of the **Capsule** GameObject
- Code flow now jumps to the `Spinner` Component object

Spinner (on the Capsule):

Line 6: `public void SpinLeft()`

- ◆ This is the `SpinLeft()` method called from the `LearningScript` object
- ◆ Line 8 in the code block is executed

Line 8: `transform.Rotate(0, 0, 60 * Time.deltaTime);`

- ◆ The `Rotate()` method on the `Transform` Component object is called which causes the Capsule to spin around the z-axis
- ◆ Notice though, that the variable named `transform` is used in the Dot Syntax statement instead of the `GetComponent<Transform>()` method
- ◆ Unity has several built-in Components, such as the `Transform` Component class
- ◆ Find the `GameObject` class in the **Scripting Reference** and notice that one of the variables is named `transform`
- ◆ Instead of having to use the `GetComponent()` method on a GameObject, Unity has provided a convenient variable already assigned the value of the `Transform` Component
- ◆ The following screenshot shows the `transform` variable described in the **Scripting Reference**:

GameObject
Inherits from Object

Base class for all entities in Unity scenes.

See Also: Component.

Variables

isStatic	Editor only API that specifies if a game object is static.
transform ◄———	The Transform attached to this GameObject. (null if there is none attached).
rigidbody	The Rigidbody attached to this GameObject (Read Only). (null if there is none attached).
camera	The Camera attached to this GameObject (Read Only). (null if there is none attached).
light	The Light attached to this GameObject (Read Only). (null if there is none attached).
animation	The Animation attached to this GameObject (Read Only). (null if there is none attached).
constantForce	The ConstantForce attached to this GameObject (Read Only). (null if there is none attached).

- ◆ The `Rotate()` method shows 3 arguments being sent to the method.
- ◆ In this example, the Capsule is rotating 60 degrees per second on the z-axis.
- ◆ Code flow now returns to the `LearningScript` object.

On LearningScript:

Line 24: `if(Input.GetKey(KeyCode.RightArrow)`

- This `if` statement checks if the user has pressed the right arrow key
- If pressed, line 26 of the code block is executed

Line 26: `capsuleGO.GetComponent<Spinner>().SpinRight();`

- This is almost an exact repeat of line 21, except the `SpinRight()` method is being called

Line 29: `if(Input.GetKey(KeyCode.UpArrow)`

- This `if` statement checks if the user has pressed the up arrow key
- If pressed, line 31 of the code block is executed

Line 31: `cubeComp.SpinLeft();`

- This is different than lines 21 and 26
- Refer back to line 13. The `cubeComp` variable already stores the reference to the **Cube** GameObject and the `Spinner` Component object, thereforeJust the variable `cubeComp` is needed in the Dot Syntax to call the `SpinLeft()` method on the **Cube** GameObject
- Code flow is similar to line 8, except that the Cube rotates now

Line 34: `if(Input.GetKey(KeyCode.DownArrow)`

- This `if` statement checks to see if the user has pressed the down arrow key
- If pressed, line 36 of the code block is executed, spinning the Cube right

Have a go hero – creating and using a new variable named capsuleComp

In `LearningScript`, lines 21 and 31 perform the same functionality of calling the `SpinLeft()` method on their `Spinner` Components. Yet the code on each line is very different. The difference is that `cubeComp` already stores a reference to the Cube's `Spinner` Component. There is no `capsuleComp` variable to store a reference to the Capsule's `Spinner` Component.

Try creating a `capsuleComp` variable and store a reference to the Capsule's `Spinner` Component. Then change lines 21 and 26 to use `capsuleComp`.

Accessing GameObjects using drag-and-drop versus writing code

Unity has a rather neat feature that allows us to assign GameObjects to variables without writing the code. It definitely has its uses, however, if it's not really necessary, I recommend assigning GameObjects in code. Why?

 Six months from now, when you are the stranger looking at your own code, you may look at it and wonder why your code looks incomplete. It's your game though, so you can create it anyway you please. I'm just saying, don't go hog wild with drag-and-drop and then later wonder what it was you were trying to accomplish.

Time for action – trying drag-and-drop to assign a GameObject

Let's change a few lines of code in `LearningScript` to show how to assign the **Capsule** GameObject to the variable `capsuleGO` using drag-and-drop.

1. Either comment out line 11 using 2 forward slashes (//), or remove it.

2. On line 6, add the access modifier `public` like this: `public GameObject capsuleGO;`

3. Save the file.

4. In Unity, select the **Main Camera** GameObject.

5. Drag the **Capsule** to the **Capsule GO** field in the **Inspector**. The following screenshot shows how this is done.

6. Click on **Play**.

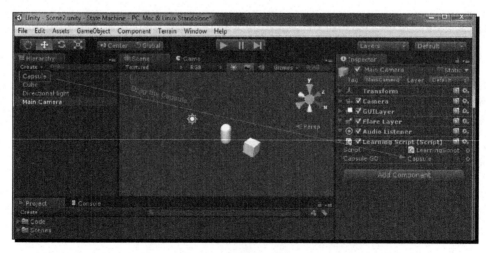

What just happened?

The **Capsule** GameObject is now assigned to the `capsuleGO` variable. We didn't have to write the code because Unity has done the assignment internally for us. Also, this doesn't change `LearningScript` in any way.

Pop quiz – understanding communication between objects

Q1. What is Dot Syntax, and what does it allow you to do?

Q2. When an object is assigned to a variable, what is actually stored in the variable?

Q3. Are there any limits to using Dot Syntax when trying to access variables and methods?

Q4. What is another way to assign GameObjects to variables besides writing code?

Summary

I hope you have discovered that Dot Syntax is actually a simple process for accessing other objects. It's this ability to communicate between objects that make OOP so powerful. Data is kept in objects, and methods are called on an object to get things done. Dot Syntax is just an address to easily access data and methods on objects.

All right, we've covered the very basics of C# scripting for Unity. Congratulations!

In the next chapter, I'm going to take you through a combination of Unity coding and general C# coding to actually apply your new knowledge. We will start looking at a State Machine to work with Unity. Yes, it's going to be a simple state machine to show the concepts. You've just barely learned C# scripting, so I'm going to ease you into some game creation which will help you see how to apply the concepts that you've just learned. Besides, bet you're darn sick and tired of constantly modifying, or completely changing `LearningScript`.

7

Creating the Gameplay is Just a Part of the Game

Gameplay is usually the main thing everyone thinks of when first undertaking the creation of a game. Build a scene, fill it with GameObjects, and write the scripts. After the game is well along in its development, a realization begins to appear that there's more to a game than just playing it. Putting a game on the market means it has to include things such as beginning title screen, the game options, or a player settings menu. Also, what happens when the user wins the game, or loses the game? It's one thing to write the code for GameObjects, but what about the code to add on all the other parts that come before and after the actual playing of the game?

In this chapter, we'll begin work on a C# State Machine, one possible solution for providing the necessary base code to easily incorporate the non-playing parts of a game.

In this chapter we will discuss the following topics:

◆ How a State Machine helps in making a game easier

◆ A logic overview of the different States

◆ The base code for creating the State Machine

So let's start to glue things together.

Applying your new coding skills to a State Machine

You learned the fundamentals of C# coding in the previous six chapters which were used for creating Components. You will use the same coding fundamentals to create a State Machine. You have learned in *Chapter 6, Using Dot Syntax for Object Communication*, that an object created from a class is called an instance of the class. In Unity, an object created from a class is called a Component. These terms may be different but they mean exactly the same; an object is created as defined by a class.

However, there is a difference in the way the traditional C# environment of the State Machine gets an instance object created, and the way Unity gets a component object created. The difference is as follows:

◆ A class we write for Unity has to be attached to a GameObject.

◆ A class we write for the State Machine is not attached to a GameObject.

◆ Unity hides the code that is necessary to create an object. Unity knows to create the object because it's attached to a GameObject.

◆ For the State Machine, we have to write the code that is necessary to create an object.

 Have no fear! It's very similar to the code in *Chapter 5, Making Decisions in Code,* we used to create a `List` and `Dictionary` object.

Understanding the concepts of a State Machine

The beauty of a State Machine lies in its simplicity, and you are already familiar with the concept. You probably spent at least the first 14 years, maybe more, of your life living in a State Machine environment; you just didn't know that it was a State Machine at the time.

As a child, your parents were always making you take a bath, go to school, do your homework, go to sleep, and whatever else you always had to do. When you were in school, you were in the school State. Were you allowed to do anything else? While sleeping, you were in your sleep State. Were you allowed to do anything else? How about the do your homework State?

The idea of being in a certain State is that you can only do what's allowed in that particular State, but you do it very well. When you put a computer program in a particular State, it will stay in that State doing only what it's supposed to do until it's told to change to another State. This is exactly what you want to do in Unity, put your game into a particular State to perform the specific behaviors you desire.

Benefits of by using a State Machine

The following are the benefits of using a State Machine:

- A very clean layout or map of the game control
- Very clear points to add game functionality or features
- Cleaner, smaller, and very specific code in each State
- It is easy to extend game logic by simply adding another State

The primary benefit of using a State Machine is for code organization. Typically, a game may start off being simple and following the code flow is easy. Unfortunately, games don't seem to stay simple. Features are added, code has to be changed with `if` statement after `if` statement added to control the game logic. It turns into a nightmare just trying to to keep track of where a specific pieces of code may be located. You'd probably add more Components to GameObjects to try to make the logic sensible. Even worse would be the use of global variables to pass data around to Components. Then you have to keep track of which Components access which global variables and hope the data stored is what you think it is at the time you access it. Trying to follow the logic ends up being like a bowl of spaghetti.

Doesn't it make sense to use the capabilities of C# to create specific State objects to keep game logic well organized, instead of attaching Components to GameObjects filled with the spaghetti code?

The following diagram is the basic concept of a State Machine for controlling a Unity project:

- Unity calls the `Update()` method every frame
- The `StateManager` script is the heart of the State Machine, a Component that has the `Update()` method
- The code block of `Update()` delegates (transfers) control to the State that is active
- States are regular C# instance objects and not GameObject Components
- The active State determines what is displayed, and therefore, is the logic controller of your game

◆ The active State decides when and which State will be active next:

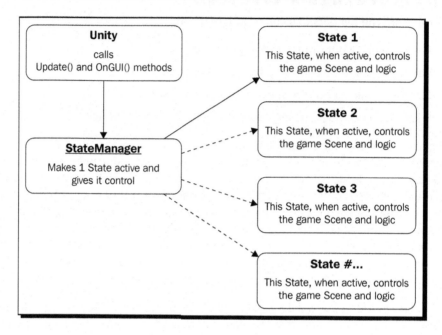

Following the State Machine logic flow

The heart of the State Machine is the `StateManager` script. This is a Unity class, so it inherits from the `MonoBehaviour` class. The script is attached to a GameObject to become a Component. The following are the three core features that the `StateManager` script handles:

◆ Delegating game control to a State

◆ Switching to another State when called to do so

◆ Keeping track of the active State

Delegating game control to a State

The `StateManager` script is like any other Unity script. It is attached to a GameObject and becomes a Component object. The `StateManager` script uses the `Update()` method to pass the game control to the active State as shown in the following diagram:

 The following diagram does not show complete code statements.

StateManager Component	Active State

`void update()`
`{`
`    activeState.StateUpdate();`
`}`
	`public void StateUpdate()`
	`{`
	`    Game code goes here`
	`}`

The game control code that's usually in an `Update()` method is instead delegated to the `StateUpdate()` method on the `activeState` object. So every time Unity calls the `Update()` method on the `StateManager` Component, the `StateUpdate()` method is called on the currently active State object.

 Please understand this principle of delegating, or transferring, responsibility from the `Update()` method of the `StateManager` script to the `StateUpdate()` method on the current active State. Believe it or not, that little bit of code is the primary driver of the State Machine's operation.

No matter how many States you may use to control your game, always remember the following points:

- Every State will have the `StateUpdate()` method, guaranteed
- The code block logic will be different for each `StateUpdate()` method on every State, depending on what you want each State to accomplish
- Only one State is active at any time

Switching to another State when called to do so

Each State determines why and when to switch to another State. You could have an almost unlimited number of reasons to switch to another State, such as losing the game, winning the game, touching some special GameObject, solving a puzzle, or the user pressing a button. No matter what the reason is, it's the code in the active State that will trigger the switch to another State.

The SwitchState() method on the StateManager script is called to accomplish this.

The following diagram does not show complete code statements.

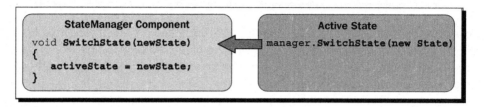

When the active State has been determined, it is time to switch to another State; the SwitchState() method on the StateManager is called. SwitchState() takes an argument of the new State, which will become active next.

Keeping track of the active State

This newly created State is then assigned to the activeState variable. Why?

In order for a State to control a game, StateManager needs to know about it. A reference of the active State object is stored in the activeState variable.

So when Unity calls Update() on the StateManager script, control is passed to the newly created State that's stored in activeState by calling its StateUpdate() method. The State Machine cycle of changing to a new State is complete.

Review the following steps:

1. The active State determines when it's time to switch to a new State.
2. A new State object is created and passed to the StateManager script using the SwitchState() method.
3. This new State object is assigned to the activeState variable.
4. When Update() is called on StateManager, the Update() method delegates control to the StateUpdate() method on the new State.
5. Now go back to step 1.

Creating Components objects and C# objects

So far in this book, you've been taught the basics of writing code to create Components for GameObjects. Incorporating a State Machine into Unity means I have to take you just a little further into the normal C# programming environment.

This will help your game coding in two ways:

- ◆ You will understand what Unity is doing behind the scenes when it creates Component objects in memory
- ◆ Making use of a C# interface will help with the game control logic

Unity creates Components behind the scenes

You already know that a Unity script is really just a file on your hard drive that defines a class. Attaching this script to a GameObject allows Unity to create a Component object in memory when you click on **Play**.

Unity hides this process of creating a Component object from your view. In my opinion, making things simple by automating processes is great because it saves time; however, it doesn't help you understand how to code.

There are third party products available that try to totally automate the code writing. Once again, this is a good thing but if you find you need to tweak or modify anything to get the exact behavior you demand, you have to get your hands dirty at some point and actually modify or write the code you need.

Well, guess what? If you don't understand how a code works, you're stuck. Learning some C# basic programming skills doesn't require a PhD in Rocket Science. If you truly want to be comfortable using Unity, knowing the basics of C# is required. You don't have to know all kinds of advanced C# coding skills to write scripts.

Look back at the material you learned in the first six chapters of this book. There wasn't anything so earth-shatteringly complicated that made you throw your hands in the air and give up. Sure, there were a bunch of words you had to learn, but everything you learned was just basic, logical steps.

Instantiate a class to create an object

Here's another new word, **instantiate**.

Not to worry, it's just a word that means create an object from a class. I've been saying create an object throughout this book. Now you have a word for it.

This is what Unity does behind the scenes when a Component is created. The script we've been using is the `LearningScript` class. When you clicked on **Play**, Unity instantiated `LearningScript` to create a `LearningScript` object which was a Component object of **Main Camera**.

We're going to leave `LearningScript` behind and start using `StateManager`, a part of the State Machine.

 Delete `LearningScript` from your `Scripts` folder in Unity.

Time for action – creating a script and a class

We are going to create the `StateManager` script and the `BeginState` class, then add some code so that we can instantiate `BeginState` to make an instance of `BeginState`. With the help of the next screenshot, perform the following steps:

1. In the Unity **Project** window, create a **C# Script** in the `Scripts` folder.

2. Name the script `StateManager`.

3. Double-click on `StateManager` to open it in MonoDevelop.

4. In the MonoDevelop **Solution** window, right-click on the `Code` folder and select **Add | New Folder**.

5. Name the folder `States`.

6. Right-click on the `States` folder and select **Add | New File**.

7. In the **New File** window, select **General | Empty Class**.

8. In the **Name** field at the bottom, enter `BeginState`.

9. Click on the **New** button to create the `class` file.

The following screenshot is the **Solution** window of MonoDevelop:

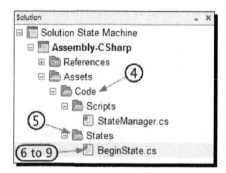

With the `BeginState` class file open in MonoDevelop, make the changes as shown in the next screenshot:

1. Change line 1 to `using UnityEngine;`.

2. Change line 3 to `namespace Assets.Code.States`.

3. Add line 9 `Debug.Log("Constructing BeginState");`.

Now the `BeginState` class file should look like the following screenshot, except for `//Constructor` on line 7 which I added as a visual aid:

```
 1   using UnityEngine;
 2
 3   namespace Assets.Code.States
 4   {
 5       public class BeginState
 6       {
 7           public BeginState ()      //Constructor
 8           {
 9               Debug.Log("Constructing BeginState");
10           }
11       }
12   }
```

Open `StateManager` in MonoDevelop, and make the following changes:

1. Add on line 2 `using Assets.Code.States;`.

2. Press *Return/Enter* so that line 3 is blank.

3. Add line 6 `private BeginState activeState;`.

4. In the `Start()` method code block, add line 10 `activeState = new BeginState();`.

5. Add line 11 `Debug.Log("This object is of type: " + activeState);`.

6. Save the file.

The StateManager class file should look like the following screenshot:

```
1 □ using UnityEngine;
2 └ using Assets.Code.States;
3
4 □ public class StateManager : MonoBehaviour
5   {
6       private BeginState activeState;
7
8 □     void Start ()
9       {
10          activeState = new BeginState();
11          Debug.Log("This object is of type: " + activeState);
12      }
13
14 □    void Update()
15      {
16
17      }
18  }
```

What just happened?

In the Unity script, StateManager, we are instantiating the BeginState class and storing a reference of (pointing to in memory) this new BeginState object in the variable activeState.

This basic process of creating objects will be used in the State Machine to switch from one State to another State. Instantiating classes is also what Unity is doing when it creates Components.

As an example, in the **Scripting Reference**, search for and select **GameObject**. You will see a variable listed named transform. When you click on **Play**, Unity instantiates the Transform class and stores a reference to the Transform Components object in the transform variable.

This means that if you need to access the data for a GameObject's Transform Components, you can simply use the transform variable instead of having to use the GetComponent<Transform>() method.

> As a little refresher, Transform is the name of the class file; transform is the name of the variable that will store a reference to the Transform object created when you click on **Play**.

This is exactly the same thing you are doing with the files you just created. The BeginState is the name of the class file. The activeState is the name of the variable that will store a reference to the to the BeginState object created when you click on **Play**.

Time for action – instantiating the BeginState class

We are going to instantiate the `BeginState` class to create an instance object in the memory. This will demonstrate how objects are created. Before we can do this, we first need to attach the `StateManager` script to a GameObject. To do so, perform the following steps:

1. Attach the `StateManager` script to the **Main Camera** GameObject.
2. Click on **Play** to show the results in the **Console** as shown in the following screenshot:

What just happened?

The `BeginState()` method in the `BeginState` class is a special method known as a constructor. It serves the same purpose as the `Start()` method or the `Awake()` method in a Unity script to initialize any member variables in the instance object created.

> A constructor method does not have a return type, not even `void`.

- I didn't have any variables to initialize, so I just sent a message to the **Console**. You could see that this method was actually called. See the first step in the previous screenshot.

- The second step in the previous screenshot shows that the value stored in the `activeState` variable is a reference to an instance object of the `BeginState` class.

The following is the code analysis on various classes:

An analysis of the code shown in the preceding code screenshot is as follows:
On `StateManager` class

Line 6: `private BeginState activeState;`

- The `activeState` is a variable that can store a reference to an object of type `BeginState`

- The `activeState` variable is private because you don't want any external code to change the stored value

Line 10: `activeState = new BeginState();`

- ◆ The `new` operator is how you create an instance of a class
- ◆ This means an instance of `BeginState` has been created in memory
- ◆ Code flow now jumps over to line 7 in the `BeginState` class

An analysis of the code shown in the preceding code screenshot is as follows:On `BeginState` class

Line 7: `public BeginState()`

- ◆ This is a constructor to initialize any member variables in the newly created instance of the `BeginState` class
- ◆ A constructor method name is the same as the class name

Line 9: `Debug.Log("Constructing BeginState");`

- ◆ This line is just sending a text message to the Unity **Console** to show that the constructor was called when the instance object was created
- ◆ This method is now finished and code flow returns back to `StateManager` line 10

An analysis of the code shown in the preceding code screenshot is as follows:On `StateManager` class

Line 10: `activeState = new BeginState();`

- ◆ A reference to the `BeginState` instance object is assigned to the variable `activeState`

Line 11: `Debug.Log("This object is of type: " + activeState);`

- ◆ This message is sent to the Unity **Console** to show you that `activeState` does reference an instance object of the `BeginState` class

Specifying a file's location with a namespace declaration

Earlier you changed line 3 in `BeginState`. What is this `namespace` on line 3?

If you look up namespace on the Internet, you might be overwhelmed with explanations. For writing classes in Unity, I'll boil it down to this:

 A `namespace` declares where a class file is located in the Unity **Project** folder structure.

For coding in the Unity environment, that's really all you need to know.

The `BeginState` file is in the `States` folder, which is a subfolder of the `Code` folder, which in turn is a subfolder of the `Assets` folder. It's a lot easier to use the Dot Syntax to express this location like this: `Assets.Code.States`. Therefore, line 3 declares this, and the whole `BeginState` class definition is in the `namespace` code block.

Now that this location has been declared in `BeginState`, any other class that wants to use `BeginState` has to specify this same location, otherwise it won't be found.

 If you move the file to a different folder, you will have to change the `namespace` as well.

Locating code files with a using statement

Look at `StateManager`. You added `using Assets.Code.States` on line 2. This means you can use any class file that resides at that location. Right now you only have `BeginState` there, but you will be adding more States later.

Introducing the C# interface

What is an interface? You might be familiar with this word. Else go ahead and look it up in a dictionary. Right! Didn't help me much either.

Let's focus on some electronic devices as examples. For example, a game controller for a game console. The buttons, the shape, and so on, that's an interface. It's how you are allowed to interact with the game. How about a TV remote? That's an interface. It's how you are allowed to control the TV. How about a smartphone? A few buttons and a touch screen, perhaps some motion. That's an interface. That's how you are allowed to use the device.

How about the Unity game engine? Does it have an interface? Sure it does. It's right there on your computer screen. It's called the **User Interface**.

There's another part of Unity that has an interface. It's called the **Scripting Reference**.

What???

Sure, think about it. In order for your GameObjects to have certain behaviors, you have to use the classes available in the **Scripting Reference**. You have certain variables and methods in each class available for you to use. That's an interface, a programmer's interface. Even more technical, it's called an **Application Programming Interface (API)**.

Every time you create a script, you get to control whether a variable is private or public. If you make it public, you have stated that the variable is an interface on that class. It even appears in the **Inspector** panel, which is another interface.

How about methods? If it's public, then it's an interface point that can be used from other classes.

The State Machine and the interface guarantee

All States have to incorporate particular methods that the `StateManger` class can call. Therefore, the States have to guarantee that these methods are implemented, otherwise the State Machine won't work.

Well, since you write the code for your classes, can't you just remember and make sure these required methods are implemented on each State? Sure, that's possible, but it's not a guarantee, is it? Suppose your game has ten possible States. There's just too much room for spelling mistakes, or just plain forgetting to implement the required methods.

C# does have a way to guarantee that the required methods are implemented in each State by using a C# `interface`. I know, I've been using the general word interface a lot here, but that's what it's called, an `interface`.

Time for action – implementing an interface

We're going to create a C# `interface` and implement it in `BeginState`, but incorrectly to see some errors. Then we'll implement the interface correctly. Perform the following steps:

1. In the MonoDevelop **Solution** window, right-click on the `Code` folder and select **Add | New Folder**.
2. Name the folder `Interfaces`.
3. Right-click on the `Interfaces` folder and select **Add | New File**.
4. In the **New File** window, select **General | Empty Interface**.
5. In the Name field at the bottom, enter **IStateBase**.
6. Click on the **New** button to create the file.

In the MonoDevelop **Solution** window, your file structure will now look like the following screenshot:

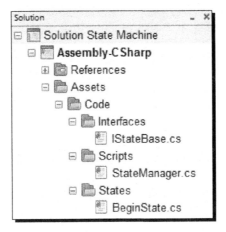

Now edit `IStateBase` file as follows:

1. Remove lines 1 and 2. As a result, `namespace` will move up to line 1.
2. Modify line 1 to: `namespace Assets.Code.Interfaces.`
3. In the `IStateBase` code block, add line 5: `void StateUpdate();`.
4. Then add line 6: `void ShowIt();`.

The `IStateBase` file will now look like the following screenshot:

```
1    namespace Assets.Code.Interfaces
2    {
3        public interface IStateBase
4        {
5            void StateUpdate();
6            void ShowIt();
7        }
8    }
```

Now we're going to have the `BeginState` class partly implementing the `IStateBase` interface so that we can see how using an `interface` guarantees our State classes meet the minimum requirements for the State Machine.

Now edit the `BeginState` class as shown in the following steps:

1. Add on line 2: `using Assets.Code.Interfaces;`.
2. Press *Return/Enter* so that line 3 is blank.
3. Modify line 6 to: `public class BeginState : IStateBase`.

We have now partly implemented the `IStateBase` interface. `BeginState` should now look like the following screenshot:

```
1 ⊟ using UnityEngine;
2 └ using Assets.Code.Interfaces;
3
4   namespace Assets.Code.States
5   {
6 ⊟     public class BeginState : IStateBase
7       {
8 ⊟         public BeginState ()      //Constructor
9           {
10              Debug.Log("Constructing BeginState");
11          }
12      }
13  }
```

4. Save your files.

5. Switch back to Unity and notice that you get two errors in the **Console**.

We were just told by Unity that we messed up. There are two errors informing us that `BeginState` did not properly implement the two methods required by the `IStateBase` interface: `StateUpdate()` and `ShowIt()`.

 This is exactly what we want the Unity to tell us. On line 6, we said we were going to use an `interface` to guarantee that all methods specified in the interface are included in our State classes. We didn't do it, so Unity let us know.

Now let's almost correct the code in the `BeginState` class:

1. Add in the two methods as shown in the following screenshot. Notice that I'm misspelling the `StateUpdate()` method as `StateUpdatee()`:

```
 1  using UnityEngine;
 2  using Assets.Code.Interfaces;
 3
 4  namespace Assets.Code.States
 5  {
 6      public class BeginState : IStateBase
 7      {
 8          public BeginState ()      //Constructor
 9          {
10              Debug.Log("Constructing BeginState");
11          }
12
13          public void StateUpdatee()
14          {
15
16          }                              misspelled
17
18          public void ShowIt()
19          {
20
21          }
22      }
23  }
```

2. Save the file.

3. Notice that Unity still let's us know that we're messing up.

4. Correct the spelling (remove the extra e from `StateUpdatee()`)

5. Save the file.

6. Click **Play** in Unity to verify that your code now works correctly.

What just happened?

The **Console** output should be exactly as it was before we created and implemented the `IStateBase` interface. Even though more methods were added to `BeginState`, there's nothing in the code blocks to execute, nor did we change `StateManager` to call the methods. Our focus was to show how to implement an interface, and how it guarantees that the interface methods for a class are included correctly.

Have a go hero – adding another method to the interface

In a later chapter, we will be adding a third method to `IStateBase` named `StateFixedUpdate()`. You may add it now if you wish. This will require you to implement the `StateFixedUpdate()` method in all States we create.

Pop quiz – using a State Machine for game control

Q1. What is the main reason to incorporate a State Machine into a game?

Q2. Since State classes aren't attached to GameObjects, how does the code in a State get executed?

Q3. How many States are allowed in a State Machine?

Q4. What should you use to guarantee that all States have the required code for the State Machine to operate properly?

Summary

We learned why a State Machine is a great way to glue the different parts of a game together, each part having it's own State of control. Then we learned a basic overview of the logic of switching States. We even took a brief glimpse into how Unity creates Components to help your understanding of code logic. Finally, we covered a way to guarantee that each State in a State Machine contains the required methods to make the State Machine work, by using a C# interface.

There are more great benefits for using a C# interface besides the programming interface it provides. In the next chapter, we get into the details of the State Machine and how the interface can work for us even more.

8
Developing the State Machine

It's time to code the State Machine so we can test its operation. We need to write the code for four initial States, the StateManager, and use the IStateBase *interface. We will first have the State Machine work with three States and then show how easy it is to add in the fourth State.*

Your Unity project may need more than four States. After you see how easy it is to add a State and how clean, simple, and organized it makes your code, your imagination may run wild on how you could make use of these States.

The whole purpose of Object Oriented Programming (OOP) is to create objects, (little packages of data) and action code (methods). In Unity, these objects are used for controlling actions in your Unity project, and they communicate with each other as well. A State Machine is simply a design choice for these objects that allows you to better organize and maintain your code.

The topics covered for the State Machine are as follows:

+ Creating State classes
+ The StateManager controller
+ The active State and Unity's Scene
+ Changing the Scenes

Well then, let's get stated...

Creating four State classes

As we create each State, you'll notice that each one is identical in structure. Again, this structure, this class interface, is guaranteed to be identical because implementing IStateBase makes it a requirement that certain methods are included in each State.

When we modify the StateManager, you'll see that it guarantees each State will implement the IStateBase interface as a requirement for being a part of the State Machine.

We already have BeginState started from the previous chapter, but it needs some modification to be functional in the State Machine. So let's modify BeginState first, and then create the other three States: PlayState, WonState, and LostState.

Time for action – modifying BeginState and add three more States

Once we modify BeginState, we'll essentially use it as a sort of template for creating all the other States, with just a few minor differences.

 I will explain code flow once we have the State Machine operating.

Using the next screenshot of BeginState, make the following changes:

1. Add line 8: private StateManager manager;.

2. Modify line 10: public BeginState(StateManager managerRef).

3. Add line 12: manager = managerRef;.

```
1  using UnityEngine;
2  using Assets.Code.Interfaces;
3
4  namespace Assets.Code.States
5  {
6      public class BeginState : IStateBase
7      {
8          private StateManager manager;
9
10         public BeginState (StateManager managerRef) //Constructor
11         {
12             manager = managerRef;
13             Debug.Log("Constructing BeginState");
14         }
15
16         public void StateUpdate()
17         {
18
19         }
20
21         public void ShowIt()
22         {
23
24         }
25     }
26 }
```

Follow these next steps three times to create the other State classes: PlayState, WonState, and LostState.

In the **Solution** window of MonoDevelop, perform the following steps:

1. Right-click on the States folder, and select **Add | New File**.
2. In the **New File** window, navigate to **General | Empty Class**,
3. At the bottom of the window, enter the class name.
4. Click on the **New** button.

In each of the three new files, make them almost identical to the code of BeginState except for the class name, the constructor method name, and the text in the Debug.Log statement.

Line 6 on each respective class file will be as follows:

* public class PlayState : IStateBase
* public class WonState : IStateBase
* public class LostState : IStateBase

Line 10 on each respective class file will be as follows:

* public PlayState (StateManager managerRef) //Constructor
* public WonState (StateManager managerRef) //Constructor
* public LostState (StateManager managerRef) //Constructor

Line 13 on each respective class file will be as follows:

* Debug.Log("Constructing PlayState");
* Debug.Log("Constructing WonState");
* Debug.Log("Constructing LostState");

 The Debug.Log statement is not a requirement in these State classes. They are only there temporarily for testing. They will be removed later.

Each State is responsible for determining why and when to switch to another State. Since there is no game code at this point, we need to manually switch States to test the State Machine. We will do this by Unity detecting when we press the Space bar key.

Add the following `if` statements to the `StateUpdate()` method code block (line 18 in the previous screenshot) for each State:

In the `BeginState` class line 18:

```
if (Input.GetKeyUp (KeyCode.Space))
  {
    manager.SwitchState (new PlayState (manager));
  }
```

In the `PlayState` class line 18:

```
if (Input.GetKeyUp (KeyCode.Space))
  {
    manager.SwitchState (new WonState (manager));
  }
```

In the `WonState` class line 18:

```
if (Input.GetKeyUp (KeyCode.Space))
  {
    manager.SwitchState (new BeginState (manager));
  }
```

In the `LostState` class line 18:

```
if (Input.GetKeyUp (KeyCode.Space))
  {
    manager.SwitchState (new BeginState (manager));
  }
```

What just happened?

We modified `BeginState` so that it would have a reference to `StateManager`, which is the controller for State switching. Once `BeginState` was properly coded, we created three more similar State classes: `PlayState`, `WonState`, and `LostState`. We now have enough code in the State classes for testing the State Machine. Now let's modify the `StateManager` class.

Setting up the StateManager controller

Now, look at line 6 of the `StateManager` class in the following screenshot. We have a big problem right off the bat:

```
 1⊟ using UnityEngine;
 2 └ using Assets.Code.States;
 3
 4⊟ public class StateManager : MonoBehaviour
 5   {
 6       private BeginState activeState;
 7
 8⊟     void Start ()
 9       {
10           activeState = new BeginState();
11           Debug.Log("This object is of type: " + activeState);
12       }
13
14⊟     void Update()
15       {
16
17       }
18   }
```

The `activeState` variable needs to be able to store all of the State types. Right now it can only store a reference to a `BeginState` type of object. This looks like a huge problem! What about the classes `PlayState`, `WonState`, and `LostState`? What if we had 50 different States that needed to be referenced in `activeState`?

The following diagram is our dilemma:

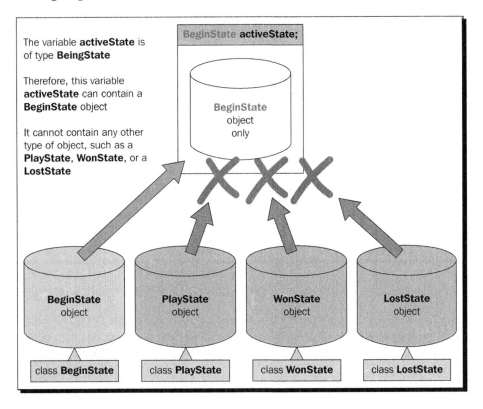

Studying an example of inheritance

Let's look at this issue using objects we all use all the time.

How about a Potato? Let's also imagine we have a Potato bag. Now to connect these real objects into the scripting world, the following is a simple declared variable:

```
public Potato bag;
```

So we have a variable named `bag`. The type of object it can store is a `Potato`. Saying this in another way: *I have a Potato bag, and the only thing I can put in it is a potato.*

The issue is shown in the following diagram:

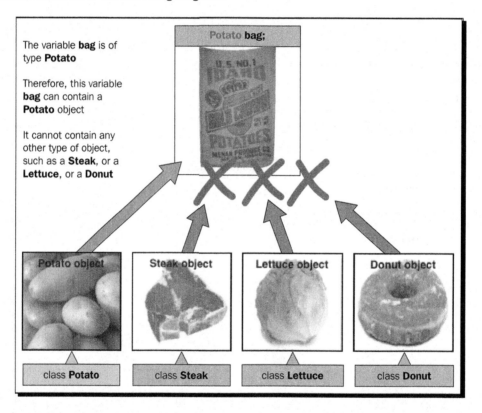

We're not allowed to put a Steak, a Lettuce, or a Donut object into a Potato bag.

This is exactly the same issue we have with our `activeState` variable that is declared to only store one type of object, a `BeginState` object. We can put a `BeginState` object in `activeState`, but not a `PlayState`, a `WonState`, or a `LostState` object.

So what do we do now?

Let's get back to the Potato example. Instead of using a very specific Potato bag, how about making the bag a bit more general, like a Food bag? Can we put a Potato in a Food bag? Is a Potato a Food? Well, we eat it, so it is a food. How about a Steak? Is that a food? Sure it is.

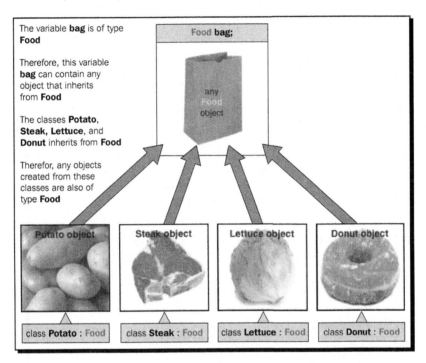

Look at each class declaration right below each Food object. Each class inherits properties from the `Food` class. Now that we're also classifying each object in the more general class of `Food`, we can now declare that the variable `bag` can hold a type of `Food`.

That's great. So, we can do something similar with our classes as well, such as create a more general `StateBase` class for the State Machine, and then modify each State class to inherit from `StateBase`, and the problem is solved. Yes, we could do that and make the State Machine work. However, inheritance does have some limitations in a State Machine and they are as follows:

- If we use inheritance, every method that's inherited will be identical, which is not what we want. The State methods need to have a code block specific to its needs.

- Using an inherited method is optional which is not what need what. We want to guarantee that the methods will be used.

- If we chose not to use an inherited method, then why bother creating the class in the first place?

◆ Also, if we created a State system using inheritance, and later wished we could inherit from more than one class, we're out of luck.

 A C# class can only inherit from one class.

The question is what to do now?

Enter the IStateBase interface again

We don't have to create another class for the State classes to inherit and get the State Machine to work.

 An interface behaves just like inheritance, plus a class can implement more than one interface.

Each of our States is already implementing the `IStateBase` interface to guarantee the methods are included. Now, since `IStateBase` acts like it's being inherited, it means each of our States can be treated as if they're an `IStateBase` type of object.

What we'll have after we modify `StateManager` is shown in the following diagram:

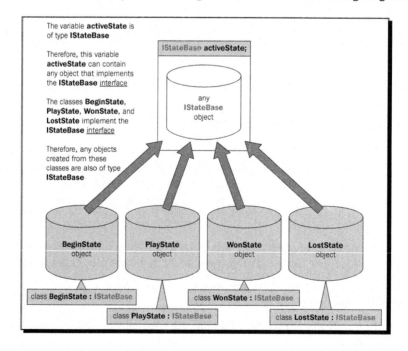

The IStateBase interface is providing a double guarantee that:

◆ The State objects will have the required methods that StateManager needs to access

◆ The activeState variable, of type IStateBase, requires all States to implement IStateBase

Time for action – modify StateManager

Edit the StateManager class to use the IStateBase interface. This allows the activeState variable to store all of the State class objects. Also add the code that does the switching to the next State:

1. Modify StateManager as shown in the next screenshot.

2. Remove the Debug.Log statement.

3. Save all files.

4. In Unity click on **Play**.

5. Now press the Space bar key to cycle through the States.

```
1  using UnityEngine;
2  using Assets.Code.States;
3  using Assets.Code.Interfaces;    ◄──── add
4
5  public class StateManager : MonoBehaviour
6  {
7      private IStateBase activeState;
8
9      void Start ()              modify
10     {
11         activeState = new BeginState(this);    ◄──── add
12     }
13
14     void Update()
15     {
16         if (activeState != null)          add
17             activeState.StateUpdate();
18     }
19
20     public void SwitchState(IStateBase newState)
21     {                                             add
22         activeState = newState;
23     }
24 }
```

What just happened?

The following is the output to the **Console** as you repeatedly press the Space bar key:

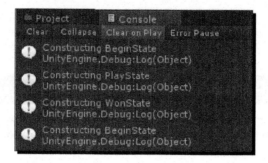

The State Machine starts with `BeginState` being active. Pressing the Space bar key makes `PlayState` the active State. Pressing the Space bar again makes `WonState` the active State, and then pressing the Space bar key once more makes `BeginState` active again.

We now have a working State Machine. For the benefits a State Machine provides, there isn't much code involved to changing States.

Let us follow the code flow for switching States:

- There are no States created as of yet
- The `StateManager` script is a Unity script, therefore Unity instantiates (creates) the `StateManager` Component object

On `StateManager`:

Line 7: `private IStateBase activeState;`

- The `activeState` variable will store a reference to a State which is an `IStateBase` type of object
- The `activeState` variable currently has a value of null, meaning there is no reference to a State object stored yet

Line 9: `void Start()`

- Unity then calls the `Start()` method, executing line 11

Line 11: `activeState = new BeginState(this);`

- The `new` keyword instantiates the `BeginState` object
- The `BeginState()` constructor method is called, and passes the argument `this` to the `BeginState` constructor

- The `this` keyword is a reference to this object, which is the `StateManager` Component object
- `BeginState` is receiving a reference to the `StateManager` object at line 11

On `BeginState`:

Line 10: `public BeginState(StateManager managerRef)`

- This is the constructor for initializing member variables
- The parameter variable `managerRef` is assigned the reference of the `StateManager` object

Line 12: `manager = managerRef;`

- The `StateManager` reference that is stored in `managerRef`, is assigned to the member variable `manager` that was declared on line 8

Line 8: `private StateManager manager;`

- The variable `manager` stores a `StateManager` type of object
- Every time a new State is created, `manager` stores a reference of the `StateManager` class, because each State needs to be able to call the `SwitchState()` method on `StateManager`

Line 13: `Debug.Log("Constructing BeginState");`

- This simply sends a text message to the Unity **Console**
- This is needed temporarily so we can see the States changing when we press the Space bar key
- The code block is now finished
- Code flow now jumps back to the place that had called this `BeginState` constructor method, which was `StateManager` line 11

On `StateManager`:

Line 11: `activeState = new BeginState(this);`

- The `BeginState` object has been created and initialized
- A reference of the `BeginState` object is now assigned to the member variable `activeState`

 At this point, `BeginState` is now the active State.

Line 14: `void Update()`

♦ This method is called every frame by Unity to execute its code block

Line 16: `if(activeState != null)`

♦ This `if` statement says that if the value in `activeState` is not equal to null, then execute

♦ Its checking to see if the variable `activeState` is storing a reference to a State object

♦ If it isn't, the value stored will be null, like it was when we first clicked on **Play**

♦ Since `activeState` is now storing a reference to `BeginState`, this `if` statement is true

Line 17: `activeState.StateUpdate();`

♦ Using Dot Syntax, the `StateUpdate()` method on `BeginState` is called every frame

♦ The code flow now jumps to line 16 of `BeginState`

On `BeginState`:

Line 16: `public void StateUpdate()`

♦ This method is called every frame by the `StateManager`

♦ There is no game to control yet, nor any game generated events

♦ Therefore, we are simply checking for a press of the Space bar key to change to another State

Line 18: `if(Input.GetKeyUp(KeyCode.Space)`

♦ Unity is checking whether we have pressed the Space bar key

♦ When we do, then the the code block is executed

Line 20: `manager.SwitchState(new PlayState (manager));`

♦ The Dot Syntax is used to call the `SwitchState()` method on `StateManager` line 20

♦ The variable `manager` stores a reference to `StateManager`

♦ The argument new `PlayState(manager)` is being passed to the `SwitchState()` method

♦ Similar to when `BeginState` was instantiated, here we have a new `PlayState` object being instantiated by using the `new` keyword

- Similar to the `BeginState()` constructor method, the `PlayState()` constructor method takes a parameter of a reference to `StateManager`, which is stored in the member variable `manager`
- Code flow now jumps to line 10 of `PlayState` to initialize it's member variables

 The code flow logic for line 10 of `PlayState` is the same as line 10 of `BeginState`.

- The argument `new PlayState(manager)` is now a reference to the new `PlayState` object just created
- It is this `PlayState` reference that is actually passed to the `SwitchState()` method on `StateManager`
- Code flow now jumps to `StateManager` line 20

On `StateManager`:

Line 20: `public void SwitchState(IStateBase newState)`

- The parameter takes the `PlayState` object reference and assigns it to the variable `newState`
- This variable stores an `IStateBase` type of object
- Remember, all States implement the `IStateBase` interface

Line 22: `activeState = newState;`

- The `PlayState` reference stored in `newState` is now assigned to `activeState`

 At this point, `PlayState` is now the active State.

Summarizing the code flow

I did a lot of explaining, but there were just the following basic things that took place after clicking on **Play**:

1. The `StateManager` object instantiated a `BeginState` object and stored its reference in `activeState`.
2. The `BeginState` object waited for us to press the Space bar key to switch States.
3. The `BeginState` object instantiated a `PlayState` object and told `StateManager` to store the `PlayState` class reference in `activeState`.

Note that steps 2 and 3 just repeat for switching to any State, no matter how many you have.

Adding another State

You've probably noticed we haven't used `LostState`. Let's see how easy it is to include another State.

Time for action – modifying PlayState to add another State

We still don't have any game logic to call for State switching, so we'll just simulate being killed in the game by detecting when the *Return/Enter* key is pressed. Add another `if` statement in the `StateUpdate()` method of `PlayState`, as shown in the following screenshot:

```
16    public void StateUpdate()
17    {
18        if (Input.GetKeyUp (KeyCode.Space))
19        {
20            manager.SwitchState (new WonState (manager));
21        }
22                                                      add
23        if (Input.GetKeyUp (KeyCode.Return))
24        {
25            manager.SwitchState (new LostState (manager));
26        }
27    }
```

What just happened?

That's it. That's all it takes to add another State. Simply call the `SwitchState()` method to instantiate any State class you wish.

The following is the **Console** output when you press *Return/Enter* while in `PlayState`:

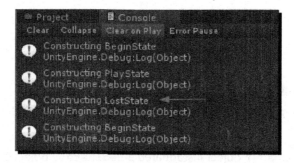

What happens if you press the *Return/Enter* key while in any of the other States? Nothing, of course. There's no code for the *Return/Enter* key in the other States.

> This maybe a simple example, but it demonstrates how each State has its own controlling game code.

Adding OnGUI to the StateManager class

The `IStateBase` interface requires that each State class have the `ShowIt()` method. The `ShowIt()` method will also be called from the `StateManager`. It's time to connect this method with the `StateManager` code.

The `StateManager` class needs to have Unity's `OnGUI()` method. Just the way the `UpDate()` method transfers control to the `StateUpdate()` method on the active State, the `OnGUI()` method transfers control to the `ShowIt()` method on the active State as well.

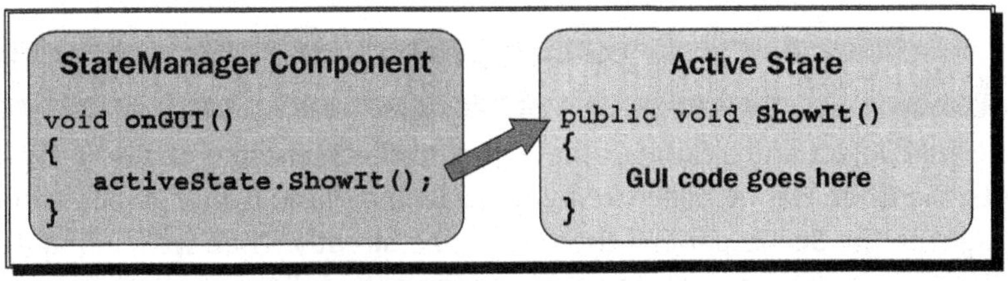

```
StateManager Component              Active State

void onGUI()                        public void ShowIt()
{                                   {
    activeState.ShowIt();               GUI code goes here
}                                   }
```

Time for action – adding OnGUI to StateManager

Add the `OnGUI()` method to `StateManager` as shown in the following screenshot. Begin the method on line 22:

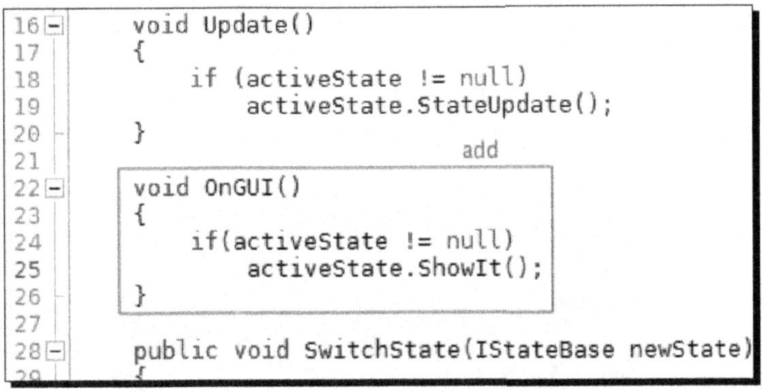

```
16      void Update()
17      {
18          if (activeState != null)
19              activeState.StateUpdate();
20      }
21                          add
22      void OnGUI()
23      {
24          if(activeState != null)
25              activeState.ShowIt();
26      }
27
28      public void SwitchState(IStateBase newState)
29      {
```

What just happened?

Unity calls the `OnGUI()` method at least once per frame, but it could also be several times per frame. This means that the `ShowIt()` method on the active State will be also called for displaying graphics, text, and buttons.

Changing the active State and controlling the Scene

Our State Machine is presently changing States in the only **Scene** we've created, which is **Scene1**. The four States we created have the names `BeginState`, `PlayState`, `WonState`, and `LostState`. However, there could be a potential issue.

Let's say you wanted `BeginState` to display a cool fullscreen graphic. The issue is that behind that graphic, your game would be active. You won't be able to see the action because of the fullscreen graphic blocking your view. This is not an ideal situation.

Time for action – adding GameObjects and a button to the Scene

Add a **Plane** GameObject and a **Cube** GameObject to the **Scene** panel. Add a **Rigidbody** Component to the **Cube** GameObject so it will fall to the **Plane** GameObject. Also add a **Directional Light** to the **Scene** panel if there isn't one already. Then we'll add a GUI button to switch to the `PlayState` object. To do so, perform the following steps:

1. In the menu, navigate to **GameObject | Create Other | Plane**.
2. In the **Inspector** panel, make sure the Position is **0,0,0** for **X,Y** and **Z**.
3. In the menu, navigate to **GameObject | Create Other | Cube**.
4. Set the values in the **Inspector** panel as shown in the next screenshot.
5. Select **Cube** in the **Hierarchy** panel.
6. In the menu, navigate to **Component | Physics | Rigidbody**.
7. In the menu, navigate to **GameObject | Create Other | Directional Light** if needed.

8. Add the following code to the code block of the `ShowIt()` method of `BeginState`:

```
if (GUI.Button(new Rect(10, 10, 150, 100), "Press to Play"))
{
    manager.SwitchState (new PlayState (manager));
}
```

What just happened?

We now have a little bit of action in the Scene. When you click on **Play**, the following screenshot will be shown:

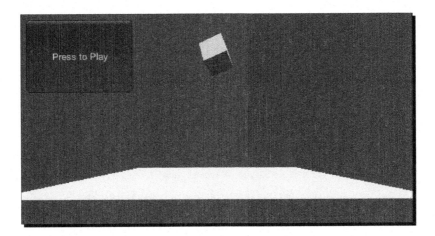

Then the **Cube** GameObject falls to the ground, **Plane**, as shown in the following screenshot:

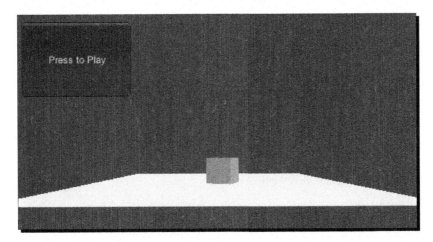

Suppose your game had many things moving around, and instead of a button, you had a fullscreen graphic. You will not see any of that movement, nor will you really want all that action taking place before you switch to the `PlayState` class.

Pausing the game Scene

There is a little trick you can use to stop all the game activity while in `BeginState`. Unity has a `Time` class and a `timeScale` variable, which you can set to slow down your game or stop it completely. It's similar to a pause feature.

Time for action – adding code to pause the game Scene

In BeginState, we're going to set timeScale to zero to pause the **Scene**. Then before switching to PlayState, we'll set it back to normal speed. Perform the following steps:

1. Modify BeginState in two places as shown in the next screenshot.

2. Save the file.

```
10    public BeginState (StateManager managerRef) //Constructor
11    {
12        manager = managerRef;
13        Debug.Log("Constructing BeginState");
14        Time.timeScale = 0;    ◄──── add
15    }
16
17    public void StateUpdate()
18    {
19        if (Input.GetKeyUp (KeyCode.Space))
20        {
21            manager.SwitchState (new PlayState (manager));
22        }
23    }
24
25    public void ShowIt()
26    {
27        if (GUI.Button(new Rect(10, 10, 150, 100), "Press to Play"))
28        {
29            Time.timeScale = 1;    ◄──── add
30            manager.SwitchState (new PlayState (manager));
31        }
```

What just happened?

An analysis of the code shown in the preceding screenshot is as follows: On the BeginState class

Line 14: Time.timeScale = 0;

♦ This line makes time in the game to stop

Line 29: Time.timeScale = 1;

♦ This sets the game speed back to normal when switching to PlayState

Click on **Play** again. Now the **Cube** GameObject is suspended in air. Click on the **Press to Play** button and everything is back to normal and you're in PlayState.

Notice how the button disappears when you change States. Once again, this shows the beauty of the State Machine. You don't have to use a bunch of if statements to make things appear or disappear. Each State determines the control you want and what shows on the screen.

Changing the State using a timer

It's great being able to stop time like that, but what if you wanted BeginState to be active for only a few seconds and then automatically change to PlayState? By setting timeScale to zero, any timers are now frozen in time.

Unity has a timer that runs, no matter what. It's a variable in the Time class called realtimeSinceStartup. When **Play** is clicked, this variable is constantly updated with the running time of the game. We can use this to create a simple timer in BeginState to make it switch to PlayState.

Time for action – creating a timer in BeginState

I've modified BeginState quite a bit just for the timer. There are now three examples of ways to switch to PlayState. Plus, there's a timer countdown displayed in the upper right corner. I also put code that I had to write more than once into a new Switch() method.

1. Edit BeginState as shown in the following screenshot.

2. Save and play in Unity.

```
1   using UnityEngine;
2   using Assets.Code.Interfaces;
3
4   namespace Assets.Code.States
5   {
6       public class BeginState : IStateBase
7       {
8           private StateManager manager;
9           private float futureTime = 0;
10          private int countDown = 0;
11          private float screenDuration = 8;                          added for timer
12
13          public BeginState (StateManager managerRef)//Constructor
14          {
15              manager = managerRef;
16              futureTime = screenDuration + Time.realtimeSinceStartup;
17              Time.timeScale = 0;
18          }
19
20          public void StateUpdate()                    added
21          {
22              float rightNow = Time.realtimeSinceStartup;
23              countDown = (int)futureTime - (int)rightNow;
24
25              if(Input.GetKeyUp (KeyCode.Space) || countDown <= 0)   modified for timer
26              {
27                  Switch();      code block modified
28              }
29          }
30
31          public void ShowIt()
32          {
33              if (GUI.Button(new Rect(10, 10, 150, 100), "Press to Play"))
34              {
35                  Switch();      code block modified
36              }
37                                                    added for displaying timer
38              GUI.Box (new Rect (Screen.width - 60,10,50,25), countDown.ToString());
39          }
40                                              method added for convienence
41          void Switch()
42          {
43              Time.timeScale = 1;
44              manager.SwitchState (new PlayState (manager));
45          }
46      }
47  }
```

What just happened?

I'm not going to walk you through the State switching code, I already did that previously.

An analysis of the code shown in the preceding screenshot is as follows: On the `BeginState` class

For lines 9, 10, and 11:

- Three member variables are declared for use in the countdown timer
- These will be explained later when they are used in code
- The reason they are declared here as member variables is that they need to be used in more than one method
- Remember the variable scope, variables are only visible within the code block they reside in

Line 16: `futureTime = screenDuration + Time.realtimeSinceStartup;`

- The `Time` class is a Unity class
- The Dot Syntax is used to access the value stored in the variable `realtimeSinceStartup`
- This variable is constantly updated with the amount of seconds the game has been running
- It stores a `float` type of value (decimal number)

> The **Scripting Reference** has a good description of `realtimeSinceStartup`, which is exactly the reason we are using it.

- The current elapsed time is retrieved from `realtimeSinceStartup` and is added with the value in the `screenDuration` variable
- The `screenDuration` variable was declared on line 11 with a value of 8 seconds, which is the length of time `BeginState` will be active before switching to `PlayState`
- The result of the addition is assigned to the variable `futureTime`
- Adding 8 seconds to the current elapsed time means I've set a time of 8 seconds into the future
- The `futureTime` variable was declared as a `float` type on line 9

Line 17: `Time.timeScale = 0;`

♦ Assigning `0` to the `timeScale` variable causes time in the game to standstill, thus pausing the game

> Both the lines 16 and 17 are executed in the `BeginState` constructor because it's only called once each time an instance object of `BeginState` is created. We want to pause the game at the instant `BeginState` is created. We also want to set the timer as well.

Line 22: `float rightNow = Time.realtimeSinceStartup;`

♦ The variable `rightNow` is declared and assigned the current elapsed time

♦ So we have `futureTime` with a value of 8 seconds into the future, and `rightNow` with a value of the actual seconds right now, which is updated constantly

♦ The value is updated constantly because the line of code is in the `StateUpdate()` method which is called constantly

Line 23: `countDown = (int)futureTime - (int)rightNow;`

♦ The difference is stored in the variable `countDown` which was declared on line 10

♦ Since `rightNow` is constantly updated, so in 8 seconds the values in `futureTime` and `rightNow` will be equal to each other

♦ Therefore, the value in `countdown` starts at 8 and decreases to 0, in 8 seconds

> Notice the `(int)` in front of each variable. The two variables are of type `float`, while countdown is of type `int`. I want it to be of type `int` when used later in line 38. The `(int)` type takes the `float` value, strips off the decimal part of the number, and leaves just an integer. A `float` is being cast (changed) to an `int`.

Line 25: `if(Input.GetKeyUp(KeyCode.Space) || countDown <= 0)`

♦ This line was modified to check two conditions using an `OR` operator

♦ When `countDown` reaches 0, this condition becomes true

♦ The code block is executed to switch to the `PlayState`

Line 27: `Switch();`

- ◆ The code that used to be here was moved to the new `Switch()` method on line 41
- ◆ This line calls the `switch()` method
- ◆ The code flow now jumps to line 43

Line 43:: `Time.timeScale = 1;`

- ◆ This line assigns the value 1 to `timeScale`
- ◆ Now the time in the game is back to normal
- ◆ Remember, we had set it to 0 on line 17

Line 44: `manager.SwitchState (new PlayState (manager));`

- ◆ This is the same switching code we always had to switch to `PlayState`, it's just in this `Switch()` method now
- ◆ Code flow now returns to line 27 where `Switch()` was called

Line 27: `}`

- ◆ The code block is finished

The following is the code flow of `BeginState` GUI:

Line 33: `if (GUI.Button(new Rect(10, 10, 150, 100), "Press to Play"))`

- ◆ Look up `GUI.Button` in the **Scripting Reference**
- ◆ It returns a Boolean (`bool`) of true when clicked
- ◆ Therefore, we use an `if` statement to detect when it's clicked
- ◆ The `Button()` method has the following two parameters:
  - ❑ A `Rect` object (rectangle) is created which specifies its position on the screen and its size
  - ❑ The `string` text that will be on the button

Line 35: `Switch();`

- ◆ This line calls the `Switch()` method on line 41

Line 38: `GUI.Box (new Rect (Screen.width - 60,10,50,25), countDown.ToString());`

- ◆ The `Box()` method creates a visible rectangle box in the **Scene** to display the timer counting down

- ◆ Because I wanted the box on the right side of the screen no matter what resolution the screen may be, `Screen.width` provides the pixel position of the right side of the **Scene**. Then I moved `60` pixels to the left of the right edge of the **Scene**.
- ◆ The `60` mean: from the last pixel on the right, come back 60 pixels to the left, and that's where to start drawing the rectangle box.
- ◆ The `countDown.ToString()` method takes an integer value stored in `countDown` and converts it to a `string` value.
- ◆ It converts it to the string value because the second parameter of the `Box()` method requires a `string` type of value.

Considering how much is going on in the **Scene**, and that there are three ways to change to `PlayState`, there really isn't very much code in `BeginState`.

When you know the syntax, how to use variables and methods, and the concept of working with objects, coding is actually quite simple to learn because you're doing the same types of thing over and over. The most difficult part of coding is trying to discover all the features that Unity provides in the **Scripting Reference**, and how they work.

You could get to know C# to the point where you dream in code, but then you have to apply that coding knowledge to Unity. So you look in the **Scripting Reference** and think what is a **EulerAngle** or a **Quaternion**? What takes time is doing the research, and not necessarily writing the code.

Have a go hero – changing the State switching order

Assuming that `BeginState` will appear when the game starts and again after you lose, change `WonState` to switch to `PlayState` instead of starting over with `BeginState`.

 Hint: you have to change only one word in the `WonState` class.

Changing Scenes

The neat thing about writing code is that there are a zillion ways to do something. Put 100 code writers in a room and tell them to make a countdown timer. You'll probably get 100 different ways to do it, and they'll all work.

So far, the State Machine is working with one **Scene** to setup game control. Well, suppose we wanted to use another, or several **Scenes**, or perhaps we don't want to use `timeScale = 0`. Of course, some changes will need to be made to work with more than one **Scene**.

Time for action – setting up another Scene

We're going to create a new **Scene** for `BeginState`. As a result, we don't want the `StateManager` object to be a Component of the **Main Camera** anymore. We'll add `StateManager` to another GameObject in the new **Scene**. In order to do so, perform the following steps:

1. Remove the `StateManager` Component from the **Main Camera**.

2. Make a new **Scene** by selecting on the menu **File | New Scene**.

3. In the menu, navigate to **GameObject | Create Empty**.

4. Rename the **GameObject** to **GameManager**.

5. Add the **StateManager** script to the **GameManager**.

6. In the menu, navigate to **File | Save Scene as...**.

7. Save the Scene as `BeginningScene` in the `Scenes` folder.

8. Click on **Play** to verify if the State Machine is working as before.

At this point, after clicking on **Play**, you will see the **Press to Play** button and the countdown timer in your Scene.

Add the Scenes to the **Build Settings** as shown in the following steps:

1. In the menu, navigate to **File | Build Settings...**.

2. In the **Build Settings** window, click on the **Add Current** button to add the `BeginningScene` to the **Scenes In Build** section.

3. Drag **Scene1** into the **Scenes In Build** section.

4. Close the **Build Settings** window.

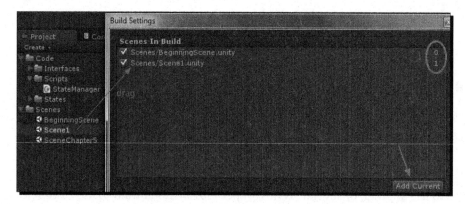

5. Edit `BeginState` to delete line 17, `timeScale = 0;`, and 43, `timeScale = 1;`.

What just happened?

By using a separate **Scene** while `BeginState` is active, there's no longer any reason to pause the game.

In the upper right corner of **Build Settings,** you can see that **BeginningScene** is index **0** and **Scene1** is index **1**. If you build this project, index **0** will be loaded automatically. It doesn't work this way in the Editor. Whatever **Scene** is loaded runs when you click on **Play**.

Changing Scenes destroys the existing GameObjects

We have two issues when using more than one **Scene** but both can be easily remedied:

◆   Every GameObject in the current **Scene** gets destroyed when another **Scene** is loaded.

When the game starts in **BeginningScene**, the **GameManager** is created with the `StateManager` Component and `BeginState` being active. When `BeginState` switches to `PlayState`, **Scene1** will be loaded and our **GameManager** will be destroyed.

◆   Every time **BeginningScene** is reloaded, another **GameManager** with another `StateManager` Component is created.

That simply isn't going to work very well. Throughout the game there needs to be only one **GameManager** with one `StateManager`.

We want the first **GameManager** with its `StateManager` Component to always be available. After all, it's the controller for the whole project. To prevent **GameManager** from being destroyed when switching from **BeginningScene** to **Scene1**, Unity provides a method called `DontDestroyOnLoad()`.

We will add this in a moment, but the second issue has to be dealt with at the same time.

In our State Machine, we have `LostState` switching back to `BeginState`. The issue is that when **BeginningScene** is reloaded, another **GameManager** GameObject will be created. We don't want another one. We just want the first one we created when we first clicked on **Play**.

This is easily remedied as well by detecting that our first **GameManager** already exist and immediately destroying any new ones that are created.

Keeping GameManager between scenes

Both of these issues will be fixed in Unity's `Awake()` method. This method is called on any Component that invokes `Awake()`, right after a Scene is loaded.

Time for action – adding the Awake method to StateManager

In the code block of the `Awake()` method, we're going to check if the **GameManager** GameObject already exists. If it doesn't, we'll save it to a variable and tell Unity not to destroy it when any other **Scene** level is loaded. If it does already exist, we'll tell Unity to destroy any new **GameManager** GameObjects created.

Insert the new code as shown in the following steps:

1. Add a new `static` variable on line 9.

2. Add the `Awake()` method at lines 11 through 22 as shown in the following screenshot:

```
 5⊟ public class StateManager : MonoBehaviour
 6   {
 7        private IStateBase activeState;
 8
 9        private static StateManager instanceRef;
10
11⊟       void Awake ()
12        {
13            if(instanceRef == null)
14            {
15                instanceRef = this;
16                DontDestroyOnLoad(gameObject);
17            }
18            else
19            {
20                DestroyImmediate(gameObject);
21            }
22        }
23
24⊟       void Start ()
```

What just happened?

An analysis of the code shown in the preceding screenshot is as follows:On the `StateManager` class

Line 9: `private static StateManager instanceRef;`

- This variable named `instanceRef` stores a `StateManager` type which is a reference to the `StateManager` object in the memory
- This is also a `static` variable
- This means, that in this example, each instance of the `StateManager` Component object that's created will share and see the same value
- It is `private` so it can't be changed from outside the `StateManager` class

Line 11: `void Awake()`

- ◆ Unity calls the `Awake()` method once after all objects in the game are loaded into memory, and before the game actually plays

Line 13: `if(instanceRef == null)`

- ◆ This `if` statement is checking whether the `instanceRef` already stores a reference to a `StateManager` Component object in the memory
- ◆ If the value is equal to `null`, meaning no reference is stored, the `if` code block is executed
- ◆ If the value is not `null`, meaning there is already a reference to a `StateManager` Component in the memory, the `else` code block is executed

Line 15: `instanceRef = this;`

- ◆ Since there's no `StateManager` Component reference stored, `this`, which stores a reference to this `StateManager`, is assigned to `instanceRef`
- ◆ This will be the case when the game has just started and the `StateManager` Component is created for the first time

Line 16: `DontDestroyOnLoad(gameObject);`

- ◆ This method tells Unity to not destroy the **GameManager** GameObject, which the `StateManager` Component is attached to when changing to another **Scene** level

Line 20: `DestroyImmediate(gameObject);`

- ◆ When **BeginningScene** is reloaded, another **GameManager** GameObject is created
- ◆ Since `instanceRef` is not null, this second instance needs to be destroyed so that only the original **GameManager** exists
- ◆ The `DestroyImmediate(gameObject)` method destroys the second copy that was just created

Changing the Scenes

Now let's write the code that will change from **BeginningScene** to **Scene1**, and back to **BeginningScene**.

Time for action – adding the code to change the Scenes

We'll add a single line of code in `BeginState` and in `LostState` to change Scenes.

1. In `BeginState`, add `Application.LoadLevel("Scene1");` into the `Switch()` method on line 42 as shown in the following screenshot:

```
40      void Switch()
41      {
42          Application.LoadLevel("Scene1");
43          manager.SwitchState (new PlayState (manager));
44      }
```

2. In `LostState`, add `Application.LoadLevel("BeginningScene");` into the `StateUpdate()` method on line 20 as shown in the following screenshot:

```
16      public void StateUpdate()
17      {
18          if (Input.GetKeyUp (KeyCode.Space))
19          {
20              Application.LoadLevel("BeginningScene");
21              manager.SwitchState (new BeginState (manager));
22          }
23      }
```

If earlier in this chapter you changed `WonState` to switch to `PlayState` instead of starting over with `BeginState`, we're ready to test our State Machine again. If you didn't, the following are the changes you need to make to `WonState`:

```
16      public void StateUpdate()
17      {
18          if (Input.GetKeyUp (KeyCode.Space))
19          {
20              manager.SwitchState (new PlayState (manager));
21          }
22      }
```

3. Save all your changes.

4. Have **BeginningScene** loaded and showing in Unity.

5. Click on **Play**.

What just happened?

You should now be changing Scenes as you go from `BeginState` to `PlayState`. To get back to `BeginState`, you have to first switch to `LostState`.

Pop quiz – understanding State Machine operation

Q1. The State classes implement the `IStateBase` interface guaranteeing certain methods are included. What is the other very important feature that the interface provides for the State Machine?

Q2. Each State has to have the `StateUpdate()` and `ShowIt()` methods. What calls these methods?

Q3. What normally happens to GameObjects when changing to another Scene?

Q4. Is this sentence true or false? Once a State Machine is setup, it can't be changed.

Verifying the code of your classes

Just in case you've had any difficulty because of constantly editing your class files, the following are the screenshots of `StateManager`, `BeginState`, `PlayState`, `WonState`, and `LostState` as they currently stand.

The following is the screenshot of the `StateManager` class:

```csharp
using UnityEngine;
using Assets.Code.States;
using Assets.Code.Interfaces;

public class StateManager : MonoBehaviour
{
    private IStateBase activeState;

    private static StateManager instanceRef;

    void Awake ()
    {
        if(instanceRef == null)
        {
            instanceRef = this;
            DontDestroyOnLoad(gameObject);
        }
        else
        {
            DestroyImmediate(gameObject);
        }
    }

    void Start ()
    {
        activeState = new BeginState(this);
    }

    void Update()
    {
        if (activeState != null)
            activeState.StateUpdate();
    }

    void OnGUI()
    {
        if(activeState != null)
            activeState.ShowIt();
    }

    public void SwitchState(IStateBase newState)
    {
        activeState = newState;
    }
}
```

The following is the screenshot of the `BeginState` class:

```
1  using UnityEngine;
2  using Assets.Code.Interfaces;
3
4  namespace Assets.Code.States
5  {
6      public class BeginState : IStateBase
7      {
8          private StateManager manager;
9          private float futureTime = 0;
10         private int countDown = 0;
11         private float screenDuration = 8;
12
13         public BeginState (StateManager managerRef)//Constructor
14         {
15             manager = managerRef;
16             futureTime = screenDuration + Time.realtimeSinceStartup;
17         }
18
19         public void StateUpdate()
20         {
21             float rightNow = Time.realtimeSinceStartup;
22             countDown = (int)futureTime - (int)rightNow;
23
24             if(Input.GetKeyUp (KeyCode.Space) || countDown <= 0)
25             {
26                 Switch();
27             }
28         }
29
30         public void ShowIt()
31         {
32             if (GUI.Button(new Rect(10, 10, 150, 100), "Press to Play"))
33             {
34                 Switch();
35             }
36
37             GUI.Box (new Rect (Screen.width - 60,10,50,25), countDown.ToString());
38         }
39
40         void Switch()
41         {
42             Application.LoadLevel("Scene1");
43             manager.SwitchState (new PlayState (manager));
44         }
45     }
46  }
```

The following is the screenshot of the `PlayState` class:

```
1  using UnityEngine;
2  using Assets.Code.Interfaces;
3
4  namespace Assets.Code.States
5  {
6      public class PlayState : IStateBase
7      {
8          private StateManager manager;
9
10         public PlayState (StateManager managerRef)    //Constructor
11         {
12             manager = managerRef;
13             Debug.Log("Constructing PlayState");
14         }
15
16         public void StateUpdate()
17         {
18             if (Input.GetKeyUp (KeyCode.Space))
19             {
20                 manager.SwitchState (new WonState (manager));
21             }
22
23             if (Input.GetKeyUp (KeyCode.Return))
24             {
25                 manager.SwitchState (new LostState (manager));
26             }
27         }
28
29         public void ShowIt()
30         {
31
32         }
33     }
34 }
```

The following is the screenshot of the `WonState` class:

```
1  using UnityEngine;
2  using Assets.Code.Interfaces;
3
4  namespace Assets.Code.States
5  {
6      public class WonState : IStateBase
7      {
8          private StateManager manager;
9
10         public WonState (StateManager managerRef)    //Constructor
11         {
12             manager = managerRef;
13             Debug.Log("Constructing WonState");
14         }
15
16         public void StateUpdate()
17         {
18             if (Input.GetKeyUp (KeyCode.Space))
19             {
20                 manager.SwitchState (new PlayState (manager));
21             }
22         }
23
24         public void ShowIt()
25         {
26
27         }
28     }
29 }
```

The following is the screenshot of the `LostState` class:

```
1  using UnityEngine;
2  using Assets.Code.Interfaces;
3
4  namespace Assets.Code.States
5  {
6      public class LostState : IStateBase
7      {
8          private StateManager manager;
9
10         public LostState (StateManager managerRef)  //Constructor
11         {
12             manager = managerRef;
13             Debug.Log("Constructing LostState");
14         }
15
16         public void StateUpdate()
17         {
18             if (Input.GetKeyUp (KeyCode.Space))
19             {
20                 Application.LoadLevel("BeginningScene");
21                 manager.SwitchState (new BeginState (manager));
22             }
23         }
24
25         public void ShowIt()
26         {
27
28         }
29     }
30 }
```

Summary

This chapter was full of options and details about using the State Machine. We started by creating four States and setting up the `StateManager` class to be the controller with the help of a C# interface. We learned how to load Scenes when switching States, and keep GameObjects from being destroyed in the process. We also covered using timers and how to pause a Scene.

For such simple code, the State Machine offers a tremendous amount of control and flexibility in organizing your game code. Let's start off the next chapter by using this State Machine to actually control a few GameObjects and change States.

9

Start Building a Game and Get the Basic Structure Running

Everything you've learned in this book up to this point has mostly been about getting to know C#, and how to use it at a relatively basic level. Unity has been used more like a helper to explain C#. The next step is to focus more on using Unity's features and let C# play the supporting role. Our goal is to tap into Unity's built-in features using your new ability to write and read C# code, in order to use the variables and methods of Unity's classes provided and documented in the Scripting Reference.

The Scripting Reference provides all the keys to providing GameObjects with action and response behaviors. Over the next two chapters, we will be adding scripts to GameObjects to create a simple game. The game itself is very basic to demonstrate how to use C# and the Scripting Reference to code some of the common game features and GameObject behaviors.

In this chapter, we'll dig into the Scripting Reference some more to write the code for changing levels or Scenes, rotating Player using the Transform class, setting the Player color and specifying number of Lives that Player will have before losing the game. All of this while under the control of the State Machine.

Here's what we'll cover:

- ◆ Unity's documentation
- ◆ Initial game setup and adding a Player GameObject
- ◆ Controlling the Player GameObject

Let's take this thing for a spin...

Easing into Unity's scripting documentation

It's great that Unity has so many classes in the Scripting Reference for us to use in a Unity project. Yet, for a beginner to scripting, even the amount of features available in the Scripting Reference can be overwhelming.

The good news is the Scripting Reference is exactly what the name implies. It's a reference. It's not meant to be a document you have to totally understand before you can begin writing scripts. A reference is a document you search when you need to know how to write the code to perform a specific task.

That's great, right? Sure it is, sort of. As a beginner, how do you know what to search for? This reminds me of school. Ask the teacher how to spell a word and the teacher always responded with "Look it up in the dictionary." Ok, but how do you find out how to spell a word in a dictionary if you don't know how to spell it to find it? I always thought the teacher's answer was rather lame and a waste of energy. I didn't want a definition, just how to spell it.

Let's assume that you wanted to **lerp** between two vectors. Say what? Now seriously, how in the world would a beginner know words like this in the first place? What the heck is a "lerp"? Would you know to search for that word in the Scripting Reference?

Obviously, most beginners wouldn't know a great deal of the terms, classes, variables, and methods available in Unity. This book is about teaching you the basics of C# so that you can understand code examples presented in the Scripting Reference, and be able to implement similar code in your Unity projects.

Right now, you are at the beginning of your coding education. Learning the fundamentals of C# coding is the easy part, it's like learning how to read and write a sentence.

Now that you can read the C# code examples in the Scripting Reference, it's time to establish a logical approach to access the information it contains. Yes, reading the Unity Manual and at least glancing through the Reference Manual is a requirement. You may understand C#, but now you also have to know how to access the power in Unity, and C# is your key to unlocking that power. The Scripting Reference is only a good reference if you have a basic understanding of what you are looking for, and that knowledge comes from reading the manuals.

 The easiest way to view Unity's documentation is to click on **Help** in Unity's menu bar.

Reading the Unity Reference Manual first

This manual provides a general overview of the main features (classes) you will be accessing while writing your code. A lot of the terminology you need to know is here. At a minimum, read and absorb the terms used and become familiar with the class names in the sections on **Physics Components**, **The GameObject**, and **Transform Component**. You will need to know class names to use the **Scripting Reference** effectively.

Finding code examples in the Scripting Reference as needed

The **Scripting Reference** contains all the example code for each class. If you already know what you're looking for, then either do a search for the word or select it from the left panel. Since there are so many classes available, knowing beforehand what you need is what makes reading the **Reference Manual** a necessity.

Setup the State Machine and add a Player GameObject

We're going to use a State Machine to control the game, so let's get some ideas of what we want:

◆ The State classes for the State Machine
◆ The `BeginState` class, which is a splash screen displayed when the game starts
◆ The `SetupState` class, which provides game options
◆ The `PlayState` classes, which are two levels of gameplay
◆ The `WonState` classes, which show a graphic and proceed to the next level
◆ The `LostState` classes, which show a graphic, and replay the level or restart the game
◆ A **Player** GameObject
◆ A script to hold game data

The following **Scenes and States** diagram shows three Scenes and nine States that we'll use to control game flow:

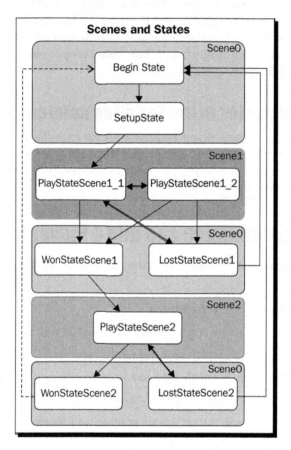

As you can see from this diagram, there are five more States and another Scene added to the project. We're almost starting fresh. Much of the code that was added in *Chapter 8* has been removed, and some new code has been added for this chapter.

 During this initial testing of the State Machine setup, the States will temporarily use the Space bar and *Return* keys for switching. Also, **Debug** information is displayed in the **Console** to show the active State.

Time for action – setting up nine States and three Scenes

We're going to modify some States and create some new ones. We're also going to use three Scenes.

In Unity

1. Create three Scenes: Scene0, Scene1, and Scene2.

2. In the menu, open **File | Build Settings....**

3. Add the three Scenes to **Scenes in Build.**

4. Temporarily add some GameObjects to **Scene1** and **Scene2** for testing.

5. Open **Scene1** and add a **Cube** GameObject.

6. Open **Scene2** and add two **Sphere** GameObjects.

7. Reload **Scene0**

8. Double-click on **BeginState** to edit

In MonoDevelop

1. Edit the BeginState constructor method as follows to add an if statement for loading Scene0:

```
public BeginState (StateManager managerRef)
{
  manager = managerRef;
  if(Application.loadedLevelName != "Scene0")
    Application.LoadLevel("Scene0");
}
```

2. Make new C# classes for the new States. The following State Machine files should be coded as shown in Appendix A:

   ❑ The BeginState file

   ❑ The SetupState file

   ❑ The PlayStateScene1_1 file: (1 of 2 available States in **Scene1**)

   ❑ The PlayStateScene1_2 file: (2 of 2 available States in **Scene1**)

   ❑ The WonStateScene1 file

   ❑ The LostStateScene1 file

   ❑ The PlayStateScene2 file

   ❑ The WonStateScene2 file

   ❑ The LostStateScene2 file

> ❑ The `StateManager` file
>
> ❑ The `IStateBase` file

3. Verify that the `StateManager` script is attached to the **GameManager** GameObject

What just happened?

You just created nine States that the game can be in. You also created three Scenes that the game will use, determined by the State the game is in.

Notice the `if` statement added in step 9. How did I know about `Application.loadedLevelName` to be able to use it?

I knew I wanted the States to control the loading of the Scenes, so how is a Scene loaded using code?

I searched the Scripting Reference using terms like scene and load. It didn't actually show exactly what I wanted, but I did see things like `Application.LoadLevelAdditive`. That sounded like what I wanted to do, so I clicked it. That provided all kinds of links, but to find everything that's available, I needed to look at the class itself. Obviously, the class name is `Application`.

Reading that page showed me the variable `loadedLevelName`. This allows me to check if the **Scene** (level) I want is loaded. If not, then `Application.LoadLevel()` is called to load the **Scene** I want for that particular State.

The following screenshot is a side-by-side view of the Project panel and the Inspector panel, showing `StateManager` as a Component of **GameManager**:

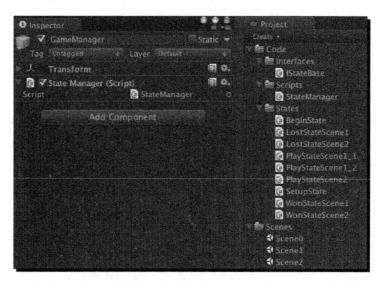

With these 11 C# classes coded, the three Scenes listed in **Build Settings**, the `StateManager` script attached to the **GameManager** GameObject, and **Scene0** loaded in Unity; you should be able to click on **Play** and see the States switch in the **Console**. As shown in the previous **States and Scenes** diagram, when you press the Space bar key and the *Return* key, watch the Scenes change in the **Game** panel.

Calling the Restart method of the StateManager

This method was added to restart the game from scratch.

◆ The `Destroy(gameObject)` method destroys the GameObject this `StateManager` script is attached to, the **GameManager**. Why destroy it?

◆ According to the State Machine, there are three places `Restart()` is called:

  ❑ At `LostStateScene1`

  ❑ At `LostStateScene2`

  ❑ At `WonStateScene2`

◆ If you have lost the game while in Scenes 1 or 2, the game needs to be restarted from scratch.

◆ If you have completed the game by winning in **Scene2**, then you're done. Restart the game.

When destroying the **GameManager**, there's no longer a State Machine, nor any data that was part of the State Machine. However, by calling `Application.LoadedLevel("Scene0")`, **Scene0** is loaded. Whenever **Scene0** is loaded, a new **GameManager** with attached `StateManager` is created because it's part of the **Hierarchy** of **Scene0**.

 Everything in a **Hierarchy** is created when a **Scene** is loaded.

So why wasn't a new **GameManager** created the other times **Scene0** was loaded, such as winning or losing in **Scene1** or **Scene2**? Actually, it was created but it was immediately destroyed since we already had a **GameManager**. See the `Awake()` method in `StateManager`. This was discussed in *Chapter 8, Developing the State Machine*.

You may be wondering if the **GameManager** is destroyed and the State Machine with it, then how could `Application.LoadedLevel("Scene0")` be called? Needless to say, I could have put this method before calling `Destroy()`, but it doesn't make any difference.

The GameObject isn't destroyed immediately. Look up **Destroy** in the **Scripting Reference** and you'll see this phrase:

> *Actual object destruction is always delayed until after the current Update loop, but will always be done before rendering.*

I can hear you saying that "`Restart()` isn't part of `Update()`." Actually it is. What called `Restart()`? We'll pick one of the three, `WonStateScene2`.

Here's the section of code calling `Restart()`:

```
public void StateUpdate()
{
  if (Input.GetKeyUp (KeyCode.Space))
  {
    manager.Restart();
  }
}
```

The `Restart()` method is called in the `StateUpdate()` method, and what calls the `StateUpdate()` method? The `StateManager` does in the `Update()` method:

```
void Update()
{
  if (activeState != null)
    activeState.StateUpdate();
}
```

As far as Unity is concerned, all this code execution happened in the `Update()` method. So once everything is finished executing as a result of `Update()` being called, the **GameManager** is then destroyed. So `Application.LoadLevel("Scene0")` was called and executed before the **GameManager** and the State Machine were destroyed.

 I didn't forget `PlayStateScene1_2`. This State will be used in *Chapter 10, Moving Around, Collisions, and Keeping Score.*

Add a Player GameObject

We need to add a GameObject named `Player` to this game. You may use any similar shaped GameObject of your choice that you have available, or simply use a GameObject such as a **Cube** added from the **GameObject** menu. The important part is that it be named `Player`.

It is going to behave like a hovercraft in the play States, so it floats above the terrain or any GameObject. In `SetupState`, we'll spin it around, select a color for it to use during the game, and set the allowed number of `Lives`.

In the following picture, on the left is the **Player** that was created using a flattened **Cube**, and a slightly stretched **Sphere**.

The **Cube** scale settings are 2, 0.5, 3. The **Sphere** scale settings are 0.32, 1.3, 0.35. The **Sphere** is a child of the **Cube**. **Cube** is renamed to **Player**. Naming it **Player** is required to have it work with the code.

On the right is a simple model I'll use just because it looks a little bit nicer than a floating brick. The model used isn't that important. The purpose of this model and the whole game is to study the C# code we will be writing.

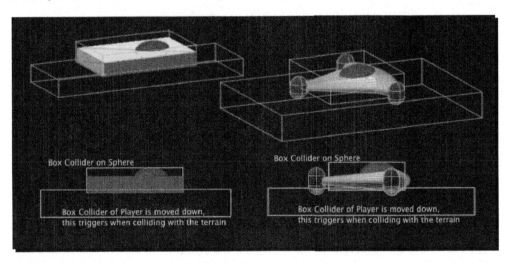

Placing and using the Player Collider

The **Box Collider of Player** is actually moved below **Player** so the collider can detect when it collides with the terrain. The **Is Trigger** property is checked. This makes a collider only detect when it collides with another collider instead of bouncing off it.

When it does detect colliding with any other collider such as the terrain or any other GameObject, **Player** will slowly rise up higher to get over it because vertical force is applied to **Player** whenever the collider is triggered.

The collider is extended a bit to the front and rear so as it moves, **Player** can rise in advance to go over small changes in the terrain, or other small GameObjects.

Placing and using the Sphere Collider

First thing to notice is that the **Sphere** isn't using a **Sphere Collider**, it's using a **Box Collider** instead. Since the **Player Box Collider** is being used for hovering, I used a **Box Collider** on the **Sphere** for **Player** to actually collide with other GameObjects, and also to prevent **Player** from ever falling through the terrain.

Time for action - adding a Player GameObject

1. Add **Player** to **Scene0**. We also need to make changes to **Scene1** and **Scene2**.

2. Click on **GameManager** and make sure its **Transform Position** is 0,0,0.

3. Add **Player** to **Scene0**.

4. Set the **Transform Position** for **Player** to 0,1,0.

5. Make **Player** a child object of the **GameManager** by dragging **Player** onto **GameManager**. Why?

   ❑ **Player** needs to be able to exist in every **Scene**

   ❑ Since **GameManager** is already allowed to exist in all Scenes as a result of the DontDestroyOnLoad() method called in StateManager, any child objects of **GameManager** will also be allowed to exist in all Scenes

6. I suggest adding **Directional Light** to **Scene0** so everything added to the Scene isn't dark.

7. Make it a child of **GameManager** as well so that all **Scene** instances will have light.

8. Save **Scene0** and load **Scene1**.

9. Remove any GameObjects in the **Scene**.

10. Save **Scene1** and load **Scene2**.

11. Remove any GameObjects in the **Scene**.

12. Finally, reload **Scene0** since this is the starting **Scene**.

What just happened?

When you click on **Play** and move from one **Scene** to another, you will see the **Player** appear in every **Scene**, along with the **Directional Light**.

Storing game data in its own script

The whole purpose of the State Machine is its simplicity of control. However, a game's code needs to access many types of data. For instance, we're going to show three splash screens. Do we really want to fill the State Machine itself with all kinds of variables storing image files and other game data? How about scoring data? Of course not, otherwise the script starts getting long and cumbersome to read.

Instead, let's create a separate Component script class whose sole purpose is to contain game data. This way we know exactly where to look for the data when we need it, and where to store it during the game. All we'll need to do is create a single variable in the StateManager that points to (references) this special data script.

Time for action – creating a GameData script

We could create a regular C# class for this, but we want to be able to assign some values in Unity's **Inspector**, so we'll create a Unity C# Script instead. There are times when you will want to use the **Inspector**, and other times, when assigning values in code is better.

To start, we are going to create three variables to store the images used for the three splash screens in `BeginState`, `WonStates`, and `LostStates`.

 By now, you should know how to create a C# Script in Unity or in MonoDevelop. From now on, you should simply create the script using whichever is most convenient at the time.

1. In the `Scripts` folder, create a new **C# Script** named `GameData`, containing the following code:

```
using UnityEngine;
using System.Collections;

public class GameData : MonoBehaviour
{
  public Texture2D beginStateSplash;
  public Texture2D lostStateSplash;
  public Texture2D wonStateSplash;

  void Start ()
  {
  }

  void Update ()
  {
  }
}
```

2. Attach this `GameData` script to the **GameManager** to make it a Component. All the data in all the variables will also persist through Scene changes.

What just happened?

Three variables are created to store the images for the splash screens. The variables store values of type `Texture2D`.

Understanding images as textures in Unity

You have to understand that Unity treats images as textures. Have a look at **Unity Manual | User Guide | Asset Import and Creation | Importing Assets**. Here's a quote:

Textures

Unity supports all image formats. Even when working with layered Photoshop files, they are imported without disturbing the Photoshop format. This allows you to work with a single texture file for a very care-free and streamlined experience.

Using splash screens between game levels

In the **Unity Manual**, there's a description on how to make a splash screen. Look in **Unity Manual | FAQ | Graphics Questions | How do I make a Splash Screen?**

However, there is an easier way by using the **GUI** system. Since an image is a texture, we'll just display our images using the `GUI.DrawTexture()` method. This draws a texture in a rectangle. We will simply make the rectangle fullscreen.

In the previous code, the three variables will each store a `Texture2D`, an image. The images are assigned to these variables by dragging the images into the **Inspector**.

 This is an example of why assigning variable values in the **Inspector** is preferred over assigning the images using code. If you ever want to change the image, it's simple in the **Inspector**, as opposed to editing code.

Displaying the splash screens

The first thing to do is import the three images you have. If you don't have anything specific already, pictures of friends or family will do nicely.

Once you have them imported, just drag them to the three variable properties in the **Inspector**. We have these texture images for our splash screens in the `GameData` Component, how do we get them to be displayed in the States we desire? By using Dot Syntax, of course. We could have each State that needs to display a splash screen, call `GetComponent()` to get the `GameData` Component.

That wouldn't be too bad with just five States needing splash screens. However, the `GameData` Component is for storing many types of data, not just splash screen images. This means that `GameData` will be accessed often for data, and calling `GetComponent()` repeatedly will slow down a game.

There is a more efficient way. Just call `GetComponent()` one time and store the `GameData` object reference that's retrieved into a variable. In fact, this is exactly what Unity suggests you do. Here's a quote from **Scripting Reference | Overview: Performance Optimization**:

3. Cache component lookups

Another optimization is caching of components. This optimization unfortunately requires a bit of coding effort and is not always worth it. But if your script is really used a lot and you need to get the last bit of performance out of it, this can be a very good optimization.

Whenever you access a component through GetComponent or an accessor variable, Unity has to find the right component from the game object. This time can easily be saved by caching a reference to the component in a private variable.

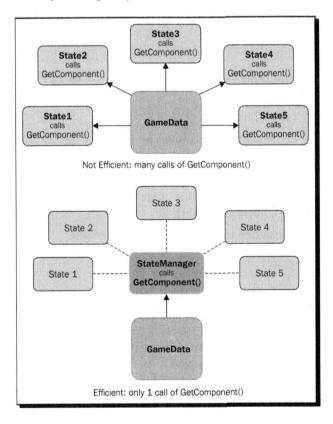

Since every State already contains a reference to `StateManager`, we will have `StateManager` call `GetComponent()` and store the `GameData` reference in a variable named `gameDataRef`. Let us have a look a the code in the following screenshot:

```
 7        private IStateBase activeState;
 8
 9        [HideInInspector]
10        public GameData gameDataRef;  ←————
11
12        private static StateManager instanceRef;
13
14 +      void Awake () ...
26
27 -      void Start ()
28        {
29            activeState = new BeginState(this);
30            gameDataRef = GetComponent<GameData>(); ←————
31        }
```

An analysis of the preceding code screenshot is given below:

In `StateManager`:

Line 10: `public GameData gameDataRef;`

- The `gameDataRef` object reference stores a reference to a `GameData` Component object
- Therefore the type is `GameData`
- It is also `public` since other classes will be accessing this variable

Line 30: `gameDataRef = GetComponent<GameData>();`

- In the `Start()` method, we call `GetComponent()` to get a reference to the `GameData` Component object
- The reference is assigned to the `gameDataRef` variable

Line 9: `[HideInInspector]`

- This is a Unity attribute that will prevent a `public` variable from showing in the **Inspector**
- Since we want the `gameDataRef` variable to only store a reference to `GameData`, there's no reason to allow it to be changed in the **Inspector**, so `HideInInspector` prevents the variable from showing

Here's the code in `BeginState` that gets the `Texture2D` image from `GameData`, then displays it on screen. It's just one line of code. I have it on three lines to fit the page:

```
17    public void StateUpdate ()
18    {
19    }      Space key detection and the call of SwitchState() removed
20
21    public void ShowIt ()
22    {
23        GUI.DrawTexture(new Rect(0, 0, Screen.width, Screen.height),
24            manager.gameDataRef.beginStateSplash,
25            ScaleMode.StretchToFill);
26
27        if (GUI.Button(new Rect(10, 10, 250, 60),
28            "Press Here or Any Key to Continue") ||
29            Input.anyKeyDown)
30        {
31            manager.SwitchState (new SetupState (manager));
32        }
33    }
```

In `BeginState`:

Line 19: Code removed.

Line 23: The `GUI.DrawTexture` method.

- The `GUI.DrawTexture()` method draws a `Texture2D` in a rectangle that is the size of the game screen
- The `manager.gameDataRef.beginStateSplash` statement is the Dot Syntax used to retrieve the image stored in the `GameData` Component
- The `manager` object reference stores a reference to the `StateManager` Component
- The `gameDataRef` variable in `StateManager` stores the reference to the `GameData` Component
- The `beginStateSplash` variable in `GameData` stores the `Texture2D` image
- This is a direct retrieval of the image since there was no need to call `GetComponent()`

Line 27: The `if` statement.

- This `if` statement is checking if a GUI button is clicked or if any keyboard key is pressed
- If either one happens, then `SwitchState()` is called to switch to `SetupState`

Here is the result when you click on **Play**, a fullscreen splash screen with a GUI button:

For our little game demonstration, the `BeginState` code is complete. There's not much to it, a little State Machine code, one line of code to display the splash screen, and a line of code to detect when to switch to `SetupState`.

The following code is the complete code of `BeginState`:

```
using UnityEngine;
using Assets.Code.Interfaces;

namespace Assets.Code.States
{
  public class BeginState : IStateBase
  {
    private StateManager manager;

    public BeginState (StateManager managerRef)
    {
      manager = managerRef;
      if(Application.loadedLevelName != "Scene0")
        Application.LoadLevel("Scene0");
    }

    public void StateUpdate ()
    {
```

```
      }

      public void ShowIt ()
      {
        GUI.DrawTexture(new Rect(0, 0,
          Screen.width, Screen.height),
          manager.gameDataRef.beginStateSplash,
          ScaleMode.StretchToFill);

        if (GUI.Button(new Rect(10, 10, 250, 60),
          "Press Here or Any Key to Continue") ||
            Input.anyKeyDown)
        {
          manager.SwitchState (new SetupState (manager));
        }
      }
    }
  }
```

Have a go hero – adjusting the button size and placement

You may find that the button size and placement isn't very good for the image you're using for the splashscreen. Try changing the button code to place it on different areas of the screen.

Controlling the Player GameObject

Let's actually begin to have our **Player** GameObject do something in the next State, `SetupState`. The **Player** GameObject will be rotating while options are displayed to set the **Player Color** and the number of **Lives** that **Player** can lose before losing the game.

We are going to create a script named `PlayerControl` and attach it to **Player**. This script will have variables and methods to manipulate the behavior of **Player**. However, the script will be controlled by the State Machine.

 If you weren't using a State Machine, the code for controlling a GameObject would usually be in the `Update()` method.

Time for action – rotating Player in SetupState

There will be a setting in the **Inspector** panel to set the rotating speed. Why is **Player** rotating in SetupState? It allows you to view the changes made to **Player**. It's also a nice visual effect, much better than just looking at a static screen.

1. Create a script containing the code shown in the following screenshot:

```
1    using UnityEngine;
2    using System.Collections;
3
4    public class PlayerControl : MonoBehaviour
5    {
6        public float setupSpinSpeed = 50.0f;   ◄────
7
8        void Start ()
9        {
10
11       }
12
13       public void PlayerUpdate ()   ◄────
14       {
15
16       }
17   }
```

2. Create a **C# Script** and name it PlayerControl.

3. Open it in MonoDevelop.

4. Add the setupSpinSpeed variable as shown on line 6 of the preceding screenshot.

5. Modify Update() as shown on line 13 of the preceding screenshot.

6. Save the file.

7. Attach this script to the **Player** GameObject.

To control the rotation of **Player**, we need to add the code (shown in the following screenshot) to SetupState.

```
1   using UnityEngine;
2   using Assets.Code.Interfaces;
3   using System.Collections;
4
5   namespace Assets.Code.States
6   {
7       public class SetupState : IStateBase
8       {
9           private StateManager manager;
10          private GameObject player;        ◄────
11          private PlayerControl controller;  ◄────
12
13          public SetupState (StateManager managerRef)
14          {
15              manager = managerRef;
16              if(Application.loadedLevelName != "Scene0")
17                  Application.LoadLevel("Scene0");
18
19              player = GameObject.Find("Player");            ◄────
20              controller = player.GetComponent<PlayerControl>();  ◄────
21          }
22
23          public void StateUpdate ()
24          {
25              if(!Input.GetButton("Jump"))
26                  controller.transform.Rotate(0, controller.setupSpinSpeed * Time.deltaTime, 0);
27          }
```

The SetupState class needs to have two pieces of information to be able to control **Player**.

- ◆ It needs to know about the **Player** GameObject
- ◆ It needs to know about the PlayerControl Component script attached to **Player**

Therefore we need two variables to store this information in SetupState. Then it's just a matter of using Dot Syntax to control the **Player**.

1. Add a variable named player as shown on line 10.

2. Add a variable named controller as shown on line 11.

3. In the SetupState() constructor method, add lines 19 and 20.

4. In the StateUpdate() method, add lines 25 and 26.

What just happened?

Let us analyze the code shown in the preceding screenshot:

In `PlayerControl`:

Line 6: `public float setupSpinSpeed = 50.0f;`

- ◆ This variable is `public` so it will appear in the **Inspector**
- ◆ It is set for a rotation speed of 50 degrees per second. Why?Just seems to be a nice speed visually

Line 13: `public void PlayerUpdate ()`

- ◆ This method needs to be `public` because it will be called from a State's `StateUpdate()` method
- ◆ Since the State Machine is controlling what code is invoked and when, `PlayerControl` won't be using the usual `Update()` method

In `SetupState`:

Line 10: `private GameObject player;`

- ◆ The variable `player` is going to store a reference to the **Player** GameObject
- ◆ It's `private` because only `SetupState` needs to see this variable

Line 11: `private PlayerControl controller;`

- ◆ The variable `controller` is going to store a reference to the `PlayerControl` Component object that's attached to **Player**

Line 19: `player = GameObject.Find("Player");`

- ◆ `GameObject.Find()` is the method used to find the **Player** GameObject
- ◆ When it finds the **Player** GameObject in the memory, a reference to it is stored in the `player` variable

Line 20: `controller = player.GetComponent<PlayerControl>();`

- ◆ The `GetComponent()` method gets the `PlayerControl` script Component that's attached to **Player** and stores a reference of `PlayerControl` in the `controller` variable
- ◆ We now have access to any `public` variables and methods in the `PlayerControl` script

Line 26: `controller.transform.Rotate(0, controller.setupSpinSpeed * Time.deltaTime, 0);`

- ◆ The `Rotate()` method causes the **Player** GameObject to spin
- ◆ `Rotate()` is a method available in the `Transform` class and it takes a `Vector3` parameter
- ◆ This means it needs to know the number of degrees of rotation for each axis: `x`, `y`, and `z`
- ◆ `transform` is a variable that stores a reference to the `PlayerControl` Transform Component object in memory
- ◆ The `x` and `z` axes are `0` because we only want **Player** to spin around the vertical **y** axis
- ◆ The `controller.setupSpinSpeed` statement retrieves the value stored, `50.0`, in the `setupSpinSpeed` variable of the `PlayerControl` script
- ◆ This is multiplied by `Time.deltaTime` to give a rotation speed of `50` degrees per second

Line 25: `if(!Input.GetButton("Jump"))`

- ◆ This `if` statement checks to see if the Space bar is not being pressed
- ◆ Notice the **NOT** operator being used (exclamation point)
- ◆ When the Space bar is not being pressed, line 26 is executed
- ◆ Open the **InputManager** from the menu by selecting **Edit | Project Settings | Input**
- ◆ Expand `Jump` and you will see that `Jump` is mapped to the Space bar

Adding the Player Color option

While **Player** is spinning, we are going to create some buttons to change its color. For my **Player**, this will change the body color. If you're using a **Cube** as a **Player** GameObject, the whole Cube will change color.

Time for action – changing the color using GUI buttons

Once again, we will add some code to PlayerControl and to the ShowIt() method of SetupState. We will be creating five GUI buttons to change colors. While we're at it, we'll also create a GUI label to tell the user to press the Space bar to pause Player rotation, and modify the button to switch States.

1. The following screenshot is of the PlayerControl script. Add the code shown in the red boxes:

```
 1  using UnityEngine;
 2  using System.Collections;
 3
 4  public class PlayerControl : MonoBehaviour
 5  {
 6      public float setupSpinSpeed = 50.0f;
 7
 8      public Color red = Color.red;
 9      public Color blue = Color.blue;
10      public Color green = Color.green;
11      public Color yellow = Color.yellow;
12      public Color white = Color.white;
13                          Assigning colors to variables
14      void Start ()
15      {
16
17      }
18
19      public void PlayerUpdate ()
20      {
21
22      }
23                          A method to assign a color to Player
24      public void PickedColor (Color playerColor)
25      {
26          renderer.material.color = playerColor;
27      }
28  }
```

2. The next screenshot is of the ShowIt() method of SetupState. Write your code as shown:

```
29      public void ShowIt ()                                SetupState ShowIt() method
30      {
31          GUI.Box(new Rect(10,10,100,180), "Player Color");
32
33          if(GUI.Button(new Rect(20,40,80,20), "Red"))
34              controller.PickedColor(controller.red);
35
36          if(GUI.Button(new Rect(20,70,80,20), "Blue"))
37              controller.PickedColor(controller.blue);
38
39          if(GUI.Button(new Rect(20,100,80,20), "Green"))
40              controller.PickedColor(controller.green);
41
42          if(GUI.Button(new Rect(20,130,80,20), "Yellow"))
43              controller.PickedColor(controller.yellow);
44
45          if(GUI.Button(new Rect(20,160,80,20), "White"))
46              controller.PickedColor(controller.white);
47
48          GUI.Label(new Rect(Screen.width/2 -95, Screen.height - 100, 190, 30),
49              "Hold Spacebar to pause rotation");
50
51          if (GUI.Button(new Rect(Screen.width/2 -100, Screen.height - 50, 200, 40),
52              "Click Here or Press 'P' to Play ") || Input.GetKeyUp(KeyCode.P))
53          {
54              manager.SwitchState (new PlayStateScene1_1 (manager));
55          }
56      }
```

What just happened?

Let us analyze the code shown in the previous two screenshots:

In `PlayerControl`:

Line 8: `public Color red = Color.red;`

- The variable `red` will store a value of type `Color`
- The `red` variable is `public` so that it will show in the **Inspector** to modify the color
- The `red` variable needs to be accessed externally by `SetupState`

Lines 9 through 12:

- These are similar to line 8, just different colors

In `SetupState`:

Line 31: `GUI.Box(new Rect(10,10,100,180), "Player Color");`

- This draws a rectangular box with a title of **Player Color**
- This provides a background for the buttons
- The example in the **Scripting Reference** is very similar

Line 33: `if(GUI.Button(new Rect(20,40,80,20), "Red"))`

- ◆ The `GUI.Button()` method draws a button on the screen with a title of **Red**
- ◆ This `if` statement detects when the button is clicked
- ◆ When the button is clicked, `GUI.Button()` returns a value of `true`
- ◆ Again, this is very similar to the example in the **Scripting Reference**

Line 34: `controller.PickedColor(controller.red);`

- ◆ Using Dot Syntax, the value stored in the variable `controller` is a reference to `PlayerControl`—the Component attached to **Player**
- ◆ The `PickedColor()` method on `PlayerControl` is called
- ◆ The argument, `controller.red`, is retrieving the value stored in the variable `red` in `PlayerControl`, which is the RGBA code for the color red
- ◆ This value is being passed to the `PickedColor()` method and assigned to the parameter variable `playerColor`

In `PlayerControl`:

Line 24: `public void PickedColor (Color playerColor)`

- ◆ This is a method we create that will perform the color changing
- ◆ It takes one parameter, `Color`, that will come from calling this method in `SetupState` (see lines 34, 37, and so on, in `SetupState`)
- ◆ This method is `public` because `SetupState` needs to access it

Line 26: `renderer.material.color = playerColor;`

- ◆ Every mesh that will be visible will have a **Mesh Renderer** Component object
- ◆ The variable `renderer` stores a reference of the **Mesh Renderer** object
- ◆ The variable `material` stores a reference of the material applied to the mesh
- ◆ The variable `color` stores the color applied to the material
- ◆ The `playerColor` variable stores the color received from `SetupState` calling the `PickedColor()` method

The color of the mesh is now set until the game restarts.

In `SetupState`:

Lines 36 through 46:

- ◆ These behave exactly the same as line 33, except the colors are different

Line 48: `GUI.Label(new Rect(Screen.width/2 -110, Screen.height - 100, 220, 40), "Hold Spacebar to pause rotation");`

◆ Lines 48 and 49 are a single statement. Since it's so long, it was put on two lines.

◆ This is just a label displayed below the spinning **Player** to let the user know to press the Space bar to pause the spinning.

Line 51: `if (GUI.Button(new Rect(Screen.width/2 -100, Screen.height - 50, 200, 40), "Click Here or Press 'P' to Play ") || Input.GetKeyUp(KeyCode.P))`

◆ Lines 51 and 52 are a single `if` statement

◆ If the **GUI** button is clicked or the *P* key is pressed, line 54 is executed to switch States

Adding the Lives option for Player

The game will be lost by the Player losing all its **Lives**. The game will start with **Player** having 5, 10, or a 1000 **Lives**. The 1000 number is just a high number so that essentially the game isn't lost, at least for a very long time. That's why I called the button **Can't Lose**.

Time for action – setting the Lives for Player

The **Lives** remaining for **Player** will be stored in a variable in `GameData`. We don't want it in `PlayerControl` because this information has no bearing on controlling **Player**.

1. As shown in the following `GameData` screenshot, add lines 10 and 11:

```
 4 ⊟ public class GameData : MonoBehaviour
 5    {
 6         public Texture2D beginStateSplash;
 7         public Texture2D lostStateSplash;
 8         public Texture2D wonStateSplash;
 9
10        |[HideInInspector]
11         public int playerLives;  ◄────────
```

2. As shown in the following `SetupState` screenshot, insert the section of code in the red box:

```
29⊟          public void ShowIt ()
30           {                                              "Player Lives" code
31              GUI.Box(new Rect(Screen.width - 110,10,100,25),
32                  string.Format("Lives left: "+ manager.gameDataRef.playerLives));
33
34              GUI.Box(new Rect(Screen.width -110,40,100,120), "Player Lives");
35
36              if(GUI.Button(new Rect(Screen.width - 100,70,80,20), "5"))
37                  manager.gameDataRef.playerLives = 5;
38
39              if(GUI.Button(new Rect(Screen.width - 100,100,80,20), "10"))
40                  manager.gameDataRef.playerLives = 10;
41
42              if(GUI.Button(new Rect(Screen.width - 100,130,80,20), "Can't Lose"))
43                  manager.gameDataRef.playerLives = 1000;
44
45              GUI.Box(new Rect(10,10,100,180), "Player Color");
```

What just happened?

Let us analyze the code shown in the preceding screenshots:

In `GameData`:

Line 11: `public int playerLives;`

- ◆ The variable `playerLives` holds the remaining **Lives** available
- ◆ This value is set using **GUI** while in `SetupState`
- ◆ As **Lives** are lost, this number will decrease toward zero

Line 10: `[HideInInspector]`

- ◆ The value in `playerLives` should not be editable in the **Inspector**

In `SetupState`:

Line 31: `GUI.Box(new Rect(Screen.width - 110,10,100,25), string.Format("Lives left: "+ manager.gameDataRef.playerLives));`

- ◆ Lines 31 and 32 are only one line of code
- ◆ A GUI Box is shown on screen with the text **Lives left:** displayed, along with the value retrieved from the `playerLives` variable in `GameData`
- ◆ The **Scripting Reference** specifies the text shown in the `GUI.Box` needs to be of type `String`

- The `string.Format()` method is C# code that makes everything in the parentheses a `String`

- The `manager.gameDataRef.playerLives` statement is retrieving the value stored in `playerLives` before being converted to a `String` for display

Line 34: `GUI.Box(new Rect(Screen.width -110,40,100,120), "Player Lives");`

- This displays a GUI Box as a background for three buttons

- The title at the top is **Player Lives**

Line 36: `if(GUI.Button(new Rect(Screen.width - 100,70,80,20), "5"))`

`manager.gameDataRef.playerLives = 5;`

- This `if` statement checks to see if a GUI Button is clicked

- When clicked, the value `5` is assigned to the variable `playerLives` in `GameData` using Dot Syntax

Lines 39 and 42:

- These are similar to line 36 except for the value assigned to `playerLives`

With all this coding complete, you should have **Scene0** looking like this when in `SetupState`:

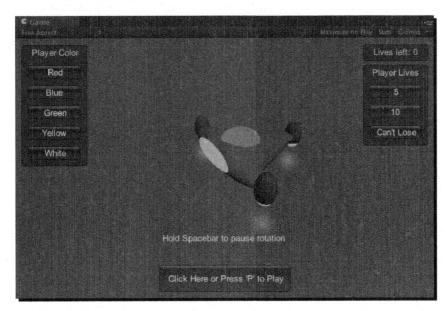

If you are using **Cube** instead, perhaps you have something like this:

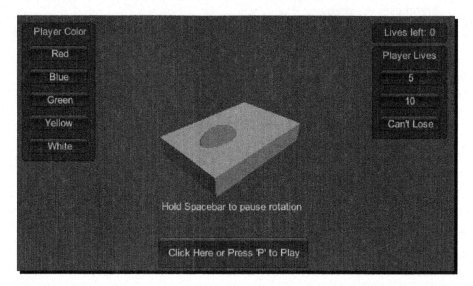

Have a go hero – changing the setup spin speed

The initial **Player** spin speed is what I happen to like. Change it to your liking in the **Inspector**, and then modify the variable in code so this spin speed will always be the default setting. Remember, changing the setting in the **Inspector** does not change any code files.

Pop quiz – understanding GameObjects

Q1. For writing scripts, what are the two primary Unity documents you should use?

Q2. What normally happens to existing GameObjects when a new **Scene** is loaded?

Q3. The States require access to data stored on GameData. Why do the States use StateManager to access this data instead of directly accessing GameData?

Q4. When **Player** is added to the **Scene** or **Hierarchy**, why is it made a child GameObject of the **GameManager** GameObject?

Summary

We looked into using Unity's **Reference Manual** and the **Scripting Reference**. As a beginner, probably the most time consuming part of writing code will be searching Unity's documentation for the information you need. We expanded the State Machine and added a **Player** GameObject. Planning ahead before writing code is always a good idea. A State Machine is a good option for organizing your project's code. Nine State classes were created for the State machine. We then displayed a splash screen and a button in `BeginState`. For the `SetupState`, we displayed a spinning **Player** and some **GUI** buttons to set **Player** options.

A major point to be taken from writing all this code is that public variables and methods in any class or script are easily accessed. All that's needed is a reference to an object, then you can use Dot Syntax to easily access data and methods.

In the next chapter, we will continue the game development by entering our first `PlayState` and see how the State Machine provides game control flexibility and code organization.

10
Moving Around, Collisions, and Keeping Score

As we enter the PlayStates, the Player needs to be able to move around in the Scene. A common way to move the Player is by using the Transform Component methods. However, we really want to use Rigidbody physics instead.

With all this moving around, it would be nice if we could always see what the Player is doing. We'll see a couple of ways the camera can keep an eye on the Player's movements.

To demonstrate game code, we'll have some good and bad GameObjects that the Player can interact with. The good objects will increase the score, and the bad objects will decrease the life of the Player.

In this chapter, we shall study:

- ◆ Starting in Scene1
- ◆ Camera views
- ◆ Moving Player using Rigidbody physics
- ◆ Keeping score
- ◆ Shooting projectiles

Let's see how all of these tie together...

Visualizing the completed game

As simplistic as this game is for learning C#, it's still nice to have some sort of picture of a game when complete. The primary goal is learning how separate pieces of code can come together to form a whole game.

The following screenshot was taken while in `PlayStatesScene1_2`. **Player** is shooting several energy pulses. Of course, your assets will probably look different, but this chapter completes all the coding necessary to have a simple functioning game.

 This chapter is going to be structured slightly differently than the previous chapters. Instead of going through step-by-step instructions to add code to our classes and scripts, all the complete files of code can be found in *Appendix B*. I will simply reference the relevant code when doing a code flow analysis.

Switching to the first play State and playable scene

Chapter 9, Start Building a Game and Get the Basic Structure Running, finished with `SetupState`. Now we need to switch to the next State, `PlayStateScene1_1`. At the bottom of the **SetupState** screen is a button **Click Here or Press 'P' to Play**.

In `SetupState`, here's the code for that button:

```
65              if (GUI.Button(new Rect(Screen.width/2 -100, Screen.height - 50, 200, 40),
66                  "Click Here or Press 'P' to Play ") || Input.GetKeyUp(KeyCode.P))
67              {
68                  manager.SwitchState (new PlayStateScene1_1 (manager));
69                  player.transform.position = new Vector3(50, .5f, 40);
70              }
```

An analysis of the code shown in the preceding screenshot is as follows:

Line 69: `player.transform.position = new Vector3(50, .5f, 40);`

◆ Places **Player** near the center of the Terrain

Loading Scene1 using code

In **Scene1**, **Player** will use physics to hover and move. Here is the relevant code in `PlayStateScene1_1`:

```
10          private GameObject player;
11
12          public PlayStateScene1_1 (StateManager managerRef)
13          {
14              manager = managerRef;
15              if(Application.loadedLevelName != "Scene1")
16                  Application.LoadLevel("Scene1");
17
18              player = GameObject.Find("Player");
19              player.rigidbody.isKinematic = false;
```

An analysis of the code shown in the preceding screenshot is as follows:

Line 15: `if(Application.loadedLevelName != "Scene1")`

◆ We were in **Scene0**, so this condition is `true`, **Scene1** is not loaded, therefore:

Line 16: `Application.LoadLevel("Scene1");`

◆ **Scene1** is loaded

Line 10: `private GameObject player;`

◆ The variable `player` will store a `GameObject` which we'll find in line 18

Line 18: `player = GameObject.Find("Player");`

◆ The `Find()` method is used to find the **Player** GameObject in the **Hierarchy**

◆ A reference to the **Player** GameObject is assigned to the variable `player`

◆ If **Player** isn't found, `player` will be storing `null` which will create an error in line 19

Line 19: `player.rigidbody.isKinematic = false;`

- With a reference to **Player**, we can access its `Rigidbody` Component stored in the variable `rigidbody`
- The variable `isKinematic` is assigned the value `false`
- The **Player** GameObject is now affected by physics in `PlayStateScene1_1` and `PlayStateScene1_2`

Adding cameras for different viewing options

Scene1 has two possible States the game can be in:

- The `PlayStateScene1_1` **State**
- The `PlayStateScene1_2` **State**

Each State will demonstrate using a different camera and a different way to keep focused on **Player** as it moves around.

Camera 1 will be positioned above and at the center of the **Terrain**. Camera 2 moves to follow **Player** around the **Scene**.

Time for action – setting up two additional cameras in the scene

We'll have three cameras, but only one will be active at a time. Their names are:

- **Main Camera**
- **LookAt Camera**
- **Following Camera**

Do the following steps with **Scene0** loaded to add two cameras:

1. Add a **Camera** GameObject and name it `LookAt Camera`.
2. Set its **Transform Position** to `50, 7, 50`.
3. Uncheck its **Active** checkbox.

4. Add a **Camera** GameObject and name it `Following Camera`.

5. Uncheck its **Active** checkbox.

6. Drag both of these cameras onto **GameManager** to make them children.

Look in the **Scripting Reference** for **GameObject.SetActive**. It's a method to set whether a GameObject is active or not. However, Unity can't find an inactive GameObject using the `GameObject.Find()` method. So we'll store a reference to each camera in a List.

Line 10 in the following screenshot of the `GameData` script creates the List to store the three cameras:

```
 4 ⊟ public class GameData : MonoBehaviour
 5   {
 6        public Texture2D beginStateSplash;
 7        public Texture2D lostStateSplash;
 8        public Texture2D wonStateSplash;
 9
10        public List<GameObject> cameras;  ◄──────
11
```

Now we'll add all the cameras in **Scene0** to the List:

1. Select **GameManager** in the **Hierarchy** panel.

2. In the **Inspector.** select **Game Data (Script).**

3. Set the **Size** of **Cameras List** to 3 .

4. Now drag the three cameras from **Hierarchy** to **Cameras Elements:**

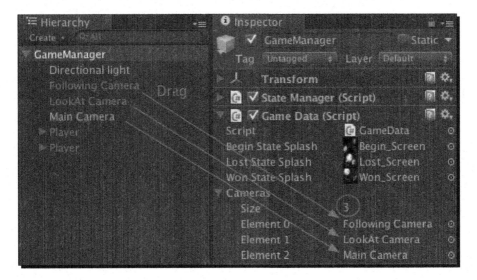

[It doesn't matter which camera is stored in any of the Elements.]

Now that we have references to all cameras, whether they are active or not, we have the ability to make a camera active in code.

1. Open `PlayStateScene1_1` in MonoDevelop.

2. Add code lines 21 through 27 as shown in the following screenshot:

```
21              foreach(GameObject camera in manager.gameDataRef.cameras)
22              {
23                  if(camera.name != "LookAt Camera")
24                      camera.SetActive(false);
25                  else
26                      camera.SetActive(true);
27              }
```

What just happened?

Let us analyze the code that we just saw:

Line 21: `foreach(GameObject camera in manager.gameDataRef.cameras)`

- This `foreach` loop retrieves each camera in the List named `cameras`
- As each camera is retrieved, it's assigned to the variable `camera`

Line 23: `if(camera.name != "LookAt Camera")`

- As the `foreach` loop iterates through the List, if the camera retrieved is not named **LookAt Camera**, then line 24 is executed
- If it is named **LookAt Camera**, then line 26 is executed

Line 24: `camera.SetActive(false);`

- This makes every camera in the List inactive if it isn't **LookAt Camera**

Line 26: `camera.SetActive(true);`

- This makes **LookAt Camera** active

Switching to `PlayStateScene1_2` makes the **Following Camera** active:

```
18              foreach(GameObject camera in manager.gameDataRef.cameras)
19              {
20                  if(camera.name != "Following Camera")
21                      camera.SetActive(false);
22                  else
23                      camera.SetActive(true);
24              }
```

As this `foreach` loop iterates though the List, **LookAt Camera** will be set as inactive, and **Following Camera** will be set to active.

Attaching scripts to the new cameras

The **LookAt Camera** and the **Following Camera** each have a script attached.

Time for actioning – attach the LookAtPlayer camera script

This simple script makes the camera look at **Player**. The camera does not move. It simply rotates so it's always looking at **Player** no matter how close or far away it is.

Attach this script to **LookAt Camera** in the **Hierarchy** panel:

```
4  public class LookAtPlayer : MonoBehaviour
5  {
6      private Transform playerPosition;
7
8      void Start()
9      {
10          playerPosition = GameObject.Find("Player").transform;
11      }
12
13      void LateUpdate( )
14      {
15          transform.LookAt(playerPosition);
16      }
17  }
```

What just happened?

Let us analyze the code that we just saw:

Line 6: `private Transform playerPosition;`

- The variable `playerPosition` will store the `Transform` information of **Player**
- This means that every frame, the `Transform` x, y, z position of **Player** is updated and stored in the variable `playerPosition`

Line 10: `playerPosition = GameObject.Find("Player").transform;`

- ◆ In order to store the `transform` position of **Player**, the script first needs a reference of the **Player** GameObject by using `GameObject.Find("Player")`
- ◆ Then the `transform` position of **Player** is retrieved and stored in the variable `playerPosition`

Line 13: `void LateUpdate( )`

Lookup **LateUpdate** in **Scripting Reference**, here's a quote:

> *...a follow camera should always be implemented in LateUpdate because it tracks objects that might have moved inside Update.*

Line 15: `transform.LookAt(playerPosition);`

- ◆ The `LookAT()` method is available in the `Transform` class
- ◆ This is the method that makes the camera's `transform` rotation change so it's always looking at the target, which is the `transform` position of **Player**

Time for action – attaching the FollowingPlayer camera script

This camera script has three added lines of code to make the camera move as **Player** moves.

Attach this script to **Following Camera** in the **Hierarchy** panel:

```
 4  public class FollowingPlayer : MonoBehaviour
 5  {
 6      public float cameraHeight = 17.0f;
 7      public float cameraDistance = 17.0f;
 8
 9      private Transform playerPosition;
10
11      void Start()
12      {
13          playerPosition = GameObject.Find("Player").transform;
14      }
15
16      void LateUpdate( )
17      {
18          transform.position = playerPosition.position +
19              new Vector3(cameraDistance, cameraHeight, -cameraDistance);
20          transform.LookAt(playerPosition);
21      }
22  }
```

What just happened?

An analysis of the code shown in the preceding screenshot is as follows:

Line 6: `public float cameraHeight = 17.0f;`

- ♦ The variable `cameraHeight` stores the distance the camera will be above **Player**

Line 7: `public float cameraDistance = 17.0f;`

- ♦ The variable `cameraDistance` stores the distance the camera will be away from **Player** on the x and z axes

Line 18: `transform.position = playerPosition.position +`

      `new Vector3(cameraDistance, cameraHeight, -cameraDistance);`

- ♦ The variable `playerPosition` stores the `transform` data of **Player**, but all we want to know is the `position` data from all that `transform` data
- ♦ Therefore, `playerPosition.position` stores the constantly changing x, y, z position of **Player**
- ♦ The height and distance data stored in `cameraHeight` and `cameraDistance` can be added to the data of **Player** to specify where the camera should be located
- ♦ The variables are plugged into the `Vector3` x, y, z positions and added to the position of **Player**

Moving the Player using Rigidbody physics

We want to add a `Rigidbody` Component to **Player**, and use gravity. Moving will be accomplished by applying a force to **Player**.

When using `Rigidbody` physics, Unity tells us to use the `FixedUpdate()` method, not the `Update()` method.

Look in **Unity Manual | Creating GamePlay | Physics**. Here's a quote:

If you move the Transform of a non-Kinematic Rigidbody directly it may not collide correctly with other objects. Instead you should move a Rigidbody by applying forces and torque to it.

Also, look in **Scripting Reference | MonoBehaviour.FixedUpdate**:

FixedUpdate should be used instead of Update when dealing with Rigidbody. For example when adding a force to a rigidbody, you have to apply the force every fixed frame inside FixedUpdate instead of every frame inside Update.

Time for action – adding a Rigidbody to the Player

We're going to add a `Rigidbody` Component to apply physics to **Player**. To stop **Player** from dropping like a rock, out of view of the camera, we'll check **Is Kinematic** in the **Rigidbody** properties to turn off the effect of physics. When any of the play States are active, we'll uncheck **Is Kinematic** in code to allow physics to affect **Player**.

1. Select **Player** in the **Hierarchy** panel.

2. At the bottom of the **Inspector** panel, navigate to **Add Component | Physics | Rigidbody**.

3. In the **Rigidbody** Component, check **Is Kinematic**.

The following screenshot shows the code for moving **Player** using physics forces:

```
 4  public class PlayerControl : MonoBehaviour
 5  {
 6      public float setupSpinSpeed = 50.0f;
 7      public float speed = 16.0f;           ⟵
 8      public float rotationSpeed = 0.60f;   ⟵
 9      public float hoverPower = 3.5f;       ⟵
10      public Rigidbody projectile;
25      void FixedUpdate()
26      {
27          float foreAndAft = Input.GetAxis ("Vertical") * speed;
28          float rotation = Input.GetAxis ("Horizontal") * rotationSpeed;
29          rigidbody.AddRelativeForce (0, 0, foreAndAft);
30          rigidbody.AddTorque (0, rotation, 0);
31      }
32
33      void OnTriggerStay(Collider other)
34      {
35          rigidbody.AddForce(Vector3.up * hoverPower);
36      }
```

What just happened?

In the **Inspector**, the values stored in the `Mass`, `Drag`, and `Angular Drag` variables under the **Rigidbody** properties affect the move ability of **Player**, just like in real life.

In any play State, **Is Kinematic** is unchecked allowing physics to work.

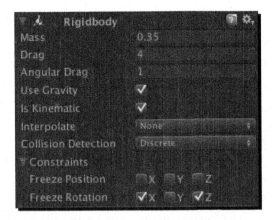

An analysis of the code we saw in the preceding code screenshot is as follows:

Note that `FixedUpdate()` is being used directly in `PlayerControl` instead of being controlled by the State Machine:

- ◆ The State Machine is controlling the `isKinematic` setting
- ◆ When `isKinematic` is checked, physics code does not work to move **Player** so there's no need to have the State Machine controlling `FixedUpdate()`

Line 7: `public float speed = 16.0f;`

- ◆ This variable will be used as a multiplier to make the forward and backward speed of **Player** faster

Line 8: `public float rotationSpeed = 0.60f;`

- ◆ This variable will be used as a multiplier to make **Player** rotate faster

Line 27: `float foreAndAft = Input.GetAxis("Vertical") * speed;`

- ◆ The `Input.GetAxis("Vertical")` method detects the pressing of the Up Arrow or Down Arrow keys
- ◆ The up arrow key returns a value of 1, while the down arrow key returns a value of -1
- ◆ These values are multiplied by `speed` which contains the value `16.0`
- ◆ The result, `16` or `-16`, is stored in the variable `foreAndAft`

Line 28: `float rotation = Input.GetAxis("Horizontal") * rotationSpeed;`

- ◆ `Input.GetAxis("Horizontal")` method detects the right or left arrow keys
- ◆ The right arrow key returns a value of `1`, the left arrow key returns a value of `-1`
- ◆ These values are multiplied by `rotationSpeed` which contains the value `0.60`
- ◆ The result, `0.60` or `-0.60`, is stored in the variable `rotation`

Line 29: `rigidbody.AddRelativeForce (0, 0, foreAndAft);`

- ◆ Since we're using the `Rigidbody` class to move **Player**, the **Scripting Reference** provides `AddForce()` and `AddRelativeForce()` for moving objects
- ◆ `AddForce()` makes objects move along the x, y, and z axes of the world, which isn't so good if **Player** isn't facing the direction where the force is being applied
- ◆ `AddRelativeForce()` makes an object move according to it's own x, y, and z axes, so applying force to the z axis of **Player** moves it correctly

Line 30: `rigidbody.AddTorque (0, rotation, 0);`

- ◆ This allows **Player** to rotate or turn

Line 33: `void OnTriggerStay(Collider other)`

- ◆ Unity automatically calls this method when a collider of another GameObject is inside **Box Collider** of **Player**

Line 35: `rigidbody.AddForce(Vector3.up * hoverPower);`

- ◆ In **Scripting Reference**, this is one of two examples to apply upward force
- ◆ This could have been written `rigidbody.AddForce(0, hoverPower, 0);`
- ◆ When the **Terrain** is inside **Box Collider** of **Player**, upward force pushes **Player** up
- ◆ As **Player** rises higher, **Terrain** gets removed from **Box Collider** of **Player**
- ◆ This removes the upward force and **Player** lowers, causing **Terrain** to be detected
- ◆ This gives **Player** the effect of hovering over the Terrain

Keeping score during the game

We have a simple system that increases **Score** of **Player** as it touches **Good Orbs** and takes **Lives** from **Player** as it crashes into **Bad Orbs**. When the **Score** reaches a set number, we win. When **Player Lives** decreases to zero, we lose.

When we lose, we have the option to retry the **Scene**. To do this, the system needs to remember what the **Score** and **Player Lives** were when first entering the **Scene** so they can be reset back to these values.

The following two screenshots show the code for initializing the score:

```
                           GameData
12          private int playerLivesSelected = 2;
13    ①     private int sceneBeginningScore;
14
15          [HideInInspector]
16          public int playerLives;
17          [HideInInspector]
18          public int score;
19
20          void Start ()
21          {
22    ②         playerLives = playerLivesSelected;
23          }
24
25    ⑥     public void ResetPlayer()
26          {
27              playerLives = playerLivesSelected;
28              score = sceneBeginningScore;
29          }
30
31    ④     public void SetPlayerLives(int livesSelected)
32          {
33              playerLivesSelected = livesSelected;
34              playerLives = livesSelected;
35          }
36
37    ⑨     public void SetScore()
38          {
39              sceneBeginningScore = score;
40          }
```

```
                          SetupState
36          if(GUI.Button(new Rect(Screen.width - 100,70,80,20), "5"))
37              manager.gameDataRef.SetPlayerLives(5);
38    ③
39          if(GUI.Button(new Rect(Screen.width - 100,100,80,20), "10"))
40              manager.gameDataRef.SetPlayerLives(10);
41
42          if(GUI.Button(new Rect(Screen.width - 100,130,80,20), "Can't Lose"))
43              manager.gameDataRef.SetPlayerLives(1000);
```

Initializing the scoring system

The following steps occur while the game is in the setup State of the game.

An analysis of the code shown in the preceding two screenshots is as follows:

In the GameData file:

Step 1:

From *Chapter 9, Start Building a Game and Get the Basic Structure Running,* we already have the variables for keeping track of the **Score** and **Player Lives** during gameplay:

- The `playerLives` variable on line 16
- The `score` variable on line 18

We need two more variables to remember the values stored in `score` and `playerLives`:

Line 12: `private int playerLivesSelected = 2;`

- The `playerLivesSelected` variable stores the **Player Lives** selected in `SetupState`
- This resets `playerLives` back to the value it was before a **Scene** is lost, or to reset `playerLives` before **Scene2** is started

Line 13: `private int sceneBeginningScore;`

- The `sceneBeginningScore` variable stores the **Score** before a **Scene** is started
- This is used to reset `score` back to the value it was before a **Scene** GameObject was lost, or to remember the **Score** earned in **Scene1** before starting **Scene2**

Step 2:

Line 22: `playerLives = playerLivesSelected;`

- When the game is started, the default value of 2 is assigned to `playerLives`

In the `SetupState` file:

Step 3:

- The user has the option to select more **Player Lives**
- Dot Syntax is used to call the `SetPlayer()` method in `GameData`
- The `SetPlayer()` method takes an argument of 5, 10, or 1000 to pass to `GameData` in line 31

In the `GameData` file:

Step 4:

Line 31: `public void SetPlayerLives(int livesSelected)`

- The value received is assigned to the parameter variable `livesSelected`

Line 33: `playerLivesSelected = livesSelected;`

- ◆ The value is assigned to `playerLivesSelected`
- ◆ The value now in `playerLivesSelected` is remembered for the whole game

Line 34: `playerLives = livesSelected;`

- ◆ The `livesSelected` variable is also assigned to `playerLives` to be displayed on screen

Keeping score in the Scene1 play State

The user has now switched from the setup State to playing the game in **Scene1**.

There are two possible play States in **Scene1**. For the scoring system, they both have the exact same code in their `StateUpdate()` methods, so I will only explain the code in `PlayStateScene1_1`.

The following screenshot shows the code for checking the **Score** to see if we win, and checking **Player Lives** to see if we lose:

```
                              PlayStateScene1_1
30        public void StateUpdate()
31        {
32            if(manager.gameDataRef.playerLives <= 0)
33    (5)     {
34                manager.SwitchState(new LostStateScene1(manager));
35                manager.gameDataRef.ResetPlayer();
36                player.rigidbody.isKinematic = true;
37                player.transform.position = new Vector3(50, .5f, 40);
38            }
39
40    (7)     if(manager.gameDataRef.score >= 2)
41            {
42                manager.SwitchState(new WonStateScene1(manager));
43                player.rigidbody.isKinematic = true;
44                player.transform.position = new Vector3(50, .5f, 40);
45            }
46        }
```

An analysis of the code shown in the preceding screenshot is given in the following subsections:

Losing the game in Scene1

In `PlayStateScene1_1` file:

Step 5:

This step is executed if we lost in **Scene1**.

Line 32: `if(manager.gameDataRef.playerLives <= 0)`

- This `if` statement checks to see if `playerLives` has decreased to zero

Line 34: `manager.SwitchState(new LostStateScene1(manager));`

- Since we lost, the State Machine switches to `LostStateScene1`

Line 36: `player.rigidbody.isKinematic = true;`

- The **Is Kinematic** option is checked to stop **Player** from being affected by physics

Line 37: `player.transform.position = new Vector3(50, .5f, 40);`

- The **Player** GameObject is repositioned back to the beginning position for **Scene1** to be replayed

Line 35: `manager.gameDataRef.ResetPlayer();`

- To replay **Scene1**, the `score` and `playerLives` variables need to be reset to the values they were when first starting **Scene1**
- The `ResetPlayer()` method in `GameData` is called in line 25

In `GameData` file:

Step 6:

Line 25: `public void ResetPlayer()`

- This resets the `score` and `playerLives` values

Line 27: `playerLives = playerLivesSelected;`

- `playerLivesSelected` is restoring `playerLives`

Live 28: `score = sceneBeginningScore;`

- `SceneBeginningScore` had a value of 0 (zero) when **Scene1** started
- This is resetting `score` back to 0

The scoring system has been reset and **Player** repositioned, ready to replay **Scene1**

Winning the level in Scene1

In `PlayStateScene1_1` file:

Step 7:

This step is executed if we win in **Scene1**.

Line 40: `if(manager.gameDataRef.score >= 2)`

- This if statement checks to see if `score` has increased to 2

Line 43: `player.rigidbody.isKinematic = true;`

- The **Is Kinematic** option is checked to stop **Player** from being affected by physics

Line 44: `player.transform.position = new Vector3(50, .5f, 40);`

- The **Player** GameObject is positioned for **Scene2**

Line 42: `manager.SwitchState(new WonStateScene1(manager));`

- Since we won, the State Machine switches to `WonStateScene1`:

```
                        WonStateScene1
10          public WonStateScene1 (StateManager managerRef)
11          {
12              manager = managerRef;
13              if(Application.loadedLevelName != "Scene0")
14                  Application.LoadLevel("Scene0");
15
16      (8)     manager.gameDataRef.SetScore();
17          }
```

In `WonStateScene1` **file:**

Step 8:

Line 16: `manager.gameDataRef.SetScore();`

- This is in the **constructor**, so as soon as the State Machine enters `WonStateScene1`, the `SetScore()` method in `GameData` is **called**

In `GameData` **file:**

Step 9:

Line 37: `public void SetScore()`

- This method is called from `WonStateScene1` line16

Line 39: `sceneBeginningScore = score;`

- The `score` variable has the value earned in **Scene1** and is the starting point for **Scene2**

Determining how to win or lose

We still need to discover the code that will increase the **Score**, or take **Player Lives**.

Player will be interacting with two simple GameObjects made using Unity's primitives, two flattened **Cylinders** and two **Spheres**.

Two versions are created, a bad GameObject with a red glowing material, and a good GameObject with a green glowing material.

Time for action – creating a good and bad prefab

We need to create two prefabs. The names aren't too important because we'll be using tags in our code. The tag names are important, which are GoodOrb and BadOrb.

1. Add two GameObjects of your choice.
2. I suggest naming them GoodOrb and BadOrb.
3. To **GoodOrb**, add a tag name of GoodOrb.
4. To **BadOrb**, add a tag name of BadOrb.
5. Create a prefab of each.
6. Randomly add about 5 of each **prefab** to **Scene1** and **Scene2**.
7. As an example, see the screenshot at the beginning of this chapter.

What just happened?

We now have the ability to increase our **Score** or lose **Lives**

Scoring for the win

All it takes to win is for the value in the variable score to be 2.

To increase score, **Player** will collide with a **GoodOrb** which increases score by 1, and **GoodOrb** will disappear from the **Scene**.

```
                        PlayerControl
38      void OnTriggerEnter(Collider other)
39      {
40          if(other.gameObject.tag == "GoodOrb")
41          {
42              gameDataRef.score += 1;
43              Destroy(other.gameObject);
44          }
45      }
```

An analysis of the code we saw in the preceding code screenshot is as follows:

Line 38: `void OnTriggerEnter(Collider other)`

 ◆ This is a copy and paste from the example code in the **Scripting Reference**

 ◆ The **Player Box Collider** is check as being **Is Trigger**

 ◆ When the **Player Box Collider** runs into the another GameObject with a **Collider**, Unity calls the `OnTriggerEnter()` method

 ◆ The variable `other` now stores a reference to the **Collider** that **Player** ran into

Line 40: `if(other.gameObject.tag == "GoodOrb")`

 ◆ We are checking to see if the GameObject that the `other` **Collider** is attached to has a **tag** named `GoodOrb`

Line 42: `gameDataRef.score += 1;C`

 ◆ `score` is increased by 1

Line 43: `Destroy(other.gameObject);`

 ◆ The `Destroy()` method is removing **GoodOrb** from the **Scene**

Losing when Player crashes

All it takes to lose is for the value in the variable `playerLives` to be 0.

To decrease `playerLives`, **Player** will collide with a **BadOrb**. The `playerLives` variable will decrease by 1, and the **BadOrb** will disappear from the **Scene**.

```
                        PlayerControl
47        void OnCollisionEnter(Collision collidedWith)
48        {
49            if(collidedWith.gameObject.tag == "BadOrb")
50            {
51                gameDataRef.playerLives -= 1;
52                Destroy(collidedWith.gameObject);
53            }
54        }
```

An analysis of the code we saw in the preceding code screenshot is as follows:

This code is similar to `OnTriggerEnter()`. However, since we are using `OnCollisionEnter()`, we have to use a **Collider** that does not have **Is Trigger** checked. The child object of **Player** is the **Sphere** which has a **Box Collider**. When this **Collider** crashes into a **BadOrb**, **Player** will lose a life.

Line 47: `void OnCollisionEnter(Collision collidedWith)`

- When **Player** runs into another GameObject with a **Collider** that is not a trigger, Unity automatically calls `OnCollisionEnter()`
- The `collidedWith` variable now stores a reference to the `other` **Collider** that **Player** ran into
- Notice that `collidedWith` is a `Collision` type, not a **Collider**
- `Collisions`, as opposed to triggers, require using the `Collision` class

Line 49: `if(collidedWith.gameObject.tag == "BadOrb")`

- This checks if the GameObject **Player** collided with has a tag named `BadOrb`

Line 51: `gameDataRef.playerLives -= 1;`

- `playerLives` is decreased by 1

Line 52: `Destroy(collidedWith.gameObject);`

- The `Destroy()` method removes **BadOrb** from the **Scene**

There is a way to increase **Player Lives**. By shooting a **BadOrb**, the variable `playerLives` will be increased by 1. It also turns a **BadOrb** into a **GoodOrb**.

Shooting projectiles at the orbs

`PlayStateScene1_1` has no code for shooting. `PlayStateScene1_2` has code to shoot one **EnergyPulse** at a time. In **Scene2**, `PlayStateScene2` has continuous rapid fire shooting.

To get the appearance of an **EnergyPulse**, we will actually shoot a **Sphere**. We won't see the **Sphere** because its rendering will be unchecked. The **EnergyPulse** effect is created by using a **Trail Renderer** effect on the **Sphere**.

Time for action – creating the EnergyPulse prefab

We need to create a prefab of our **EnergyPulse** projectile. Use the following screenshot of the **Inspector** as a guide for these steps.

1. Create a new prefab by navigating to **Assets | Create | Prefab** and name it `EnergyPulse`.
2. Add a **Sphere** to the **Scene**.
3. Position its **Transform** to 0, 0, 0.

4. Scale its **Transform** to `0.5, 0.5, 0.5`.

5. On the **Sphere Collider**, check **Is Trigger**.

6. Uncheck **Mesh Renderer**.

7. Add a **Rigidbody** Component.

8. Turn off **Gravity**.

9. Add the script `EnergyPulsePower` (see *Appendix B*).

10. Add a **Trail Renderer** Component by navigating to **Component | Effects | Trail Renderer**.

11. Drag a **GoodOrb** prefab to the **Good Orb** property on the **Energy Pulse Power (Script)**.

12. Set the **Trail Renderer** properties as shown in the following screenshot.

13. Drag **Sphere** onto the newly created, empty **EnergyPulse** prefab.

14. Now delete **Sphere** from **Scene**

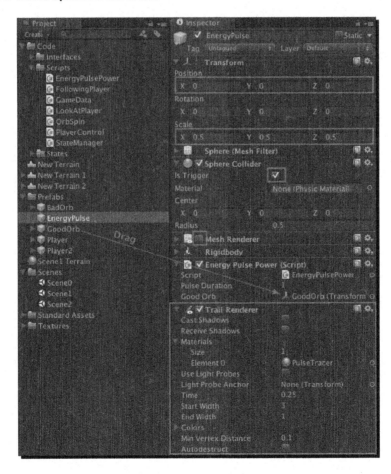

What just happened?

Now that we have our **EnergyPulse** to shoot, we can shoot them in two States:
`PlayStateScene1_2` and `PlayStateScene2`.

Shooting a single-shot EnergyPulse

`PlayStateScene1_2` only allows a single shot to be fired for each press of the key.

```
                        PlayStateScene1_2
44          if(Input.GetKeyDown(KeyCode.LeftControl))
45          {
46              controller.FireEnergyPulse();
47          }
```

An analysis of the code we saw in the preceding code screenshot is as follows:

Line 44: `if(Input.GetKeyDown(KeyCode.LeftControl))`

- ◆ The `GetKeyDown()` method means one shot will be fired every time the left *Ctrl* key is pressed

Line 46: `controller.FireEnergyPulse();`

- ◆ `FireEnergyPulse()` in `PlayerControl`, line 56, is called to fire an **EnergyPulse**

Shooting rapid-fire EnergyPulses

`PlayStateScene2` allows for continuous firing by holding the Left *Ctrl* key down.

```
                        PlayStateScene2
47          if(Input.GetKey(KeyCode.LeftControl))
48          {
49              controller.FireEnergyPulse();
50          }
```

An analysis of the code we saw in the preceding code screenshot is as follows:

Line 47: `if(Input.GetKey(KeyCode.LeftControl))`

- ◆ The `GetKey()` method means shots will be fired continuously when the left *Ctrl* key is pressed down

Line 49: `controller.FireEnergyPulse();`

- ◆ The `FireEnergyPulse()` method in `PlayerControl`, line 56, is called to fire an **EnergyPulse**

The EnergyPulse is fired

In `PlayerControl`, the **EnergyPulse** is instantiated in front of **Player**, and force is used to propel it forward. The **EnergyPulse** has to be instantiated in front of **Player** so that the **EnergyPulse Collider** doesn't detect the **Player Collider** immediately after being instantiated. If it does detect it, the **EnergyPulse** will be destroyed immediately.

The `PlayerControl` script needs to know about the **EnergyPulse** prefab so that it can be created in code. Drag the **EnergyPulse** prefab to the **Projectile** variable property in the **Inspector**:

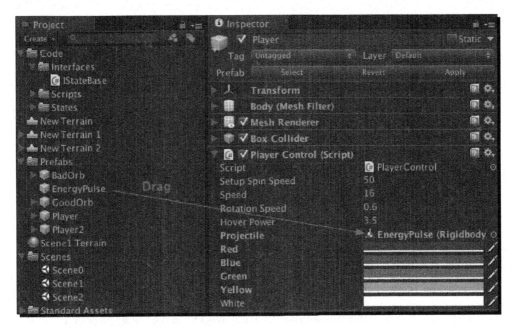

```
                                PlayerControl
10      public Rigidbody projectile;
56      public void FireEnergyPulse()
57      {
58          Rigidbody clone;
59          clone = Instantiate(projectile, transform.position, transform.rotation) as Rigidbody;
60          clone.transform.Translate(0, .5f, 2.1f);
61          clone.velocity = transform.TransformDirection(Vector3.forward * 50);
62      }
```

An analysis of the code we saw in the preceding code screenshot is as follows:

Line 10: `public Rigidbody projectile;`

- `projectile` stores the **EnergyPulse** prefab so it can be instantiated

Line 56: `public void FireEnergyPulse()`

- This is called by `PlayStateScene1_2`, **line 46**, or `PlayStateScene2`, **line 49**

Line 58: `Rigidbody clone;`

- `clone` stores a reference to the new `Rigidbody` object about to be created
- Since we will be using physics force to propel the **EnergyPulse** forward, the variable `clone` is of type `Rigidbody`

Line 59: `clone = Instantiate(projectile, transform.position, transform.rotation) as Rigidbody;`

- The `Instantiate()` method takes the **Prefab** stored in the variable `projectile` and creates an **EnergyPulse** GameObject
- The method also places in it at the same position as **Player** but we'll fix this
- Since the variable `clone` stores a `Rigidbody` type of object, and **EnergyPulse** is of type `GameObject`, **EnergyPulse** has to be converted to a `Rigidbody` type
- The `as` operator will cast (convert) the GameObject to a Rigidbody

Line 60: `clone.transform.Translate(0, .5f, 2.1f);`

- Since we can't have the **EnergyPulse** object at the same position as **Player**, `Translate()` moves it in front of **Player** before the frame is ready to display

Line 61: `clone.velocity = transform.TransformDirection(Vector3.forward * 50);`

- This sets the `force` of `Rigidbody` being applied to move **EnergyPulse** forward

We now have our **EnergyPulse** being fired. Now we need to make things happen when it hits something.

Controlling EnergyPulse objects

So **Player** shoots out this **EnergyPulse**, what happens next? Does it just go on forever? What happens if it hits something?

We certainly don't want these instantiated **EnergyPulse** Gameobjects hanging around forever. Once they've served their purpose, they should be destroyed. That's exactly what we do. After a set time, they simply disappear.

The **EnergyPulse** is meant to do two things:

- Increase **Player Lives**
- Convert a **BadOrb** into a **GoodOrb**

Anything else they hit is immune to the effects of the **EnergyPulse**. The following screenshot shows how this is done:

```
 4  public class EnergyPulsePower : MonoBehaviour
 5  {
 6      public float pulseDuration = 1f;
 7
 8      public Transform goodOrb;
 9
10      void Update()
11      {
12          pulseDuration -= Time.deltaTime;
13
14          if(pulseDuration <= 0)
15              Destroy(gameObject);
16      }
17
18      void OnTriggerEnter(Collider other)
19      {
20          if(other.gameObject.tag == "BadOrb")
21          {
22              Instantiate(goodOrb, other.transform.position, other.transform.rotation);
23              GameObject.Find("GameManager").GetComponent<GameData>().playerLives += 1;
24              Destroy(other.gameObject);
25              Destroy(gameObject);
26          }
27          else
28              Destroy(gameObject);
29      }
30  }
```

An analysis of the code we saw in the preceding code screenshot is as follows:

The `EnergyPulsePower` script is attached to the **EnergyPulse** GameObject.

Line 6: `public float pulseDuration = 1f;`

- This sets how long an **EnergyPulse** will exist
- This time is adjustable in the **Inspector**

Line 12: `pulseDuration -= Time.deltaTime;`

- This is a countdown timer that operates at the rate of `1.0` per second

Line 14: `if(pulseDuration <= 0)`

- When the value in `pulseDuration` reaches `0`, line 15 is executed

Line 15: `Destroy(gameObject);`

- Since this script is attached to the **EnergyPulse** GameObject, this **EnergyPulse** is destroyed when the timer reaches 0

That makes sure an **EnergyPulse** does not last forever.

Now we look into increasing **Player Lives** and converting **BadOrbs** into **GoodOrbs**. What happens is that a **BadOrb** collides with an **EnergyPulse**. The **BadOrb** is destroyed and disappears. A new **GoodOrb** is instantiated and placed exactly where the **BadOrb** used to be, giving the appearance that it was converted.

Line 8: `public Transform goodOrb;`

- The `goodOrb` variable stores the **GoodOrb** prefab so it can be instantiated

Line 18: `void OnTriggerEnter(Collider other)`

- This method is called by Unity when the **Sphere Collider** of the **EnergyPulse** hits any GameObject with a **Collider**
- The `other` variable now stores a reference to the **Collider** of the GameObject that was hit

Line 20: `if(other.gameObject.tag == "BadOrb")`

- If the hit GameObject's tag is `BadOrb`, then the code block is executed
- If it does not have a tag of `BadOrb`, then line 28 is executed

Line 22: `Instantiate(goodOrb, other.transform.position, other.transform.rotation);`

- **GoodOrb** is instantiated and placed right where **BadOrb** is located

Line 23: `GameObject.Find("GameManager"). GetComponent<GameData>(). playerLives += 1;`

- This finds the variable `playerLives` in `GameData` and adds 1 to it, increasing **Player Lives**

Line 24: `Destroy(other.gameObject);`

- ◆ This destroys the **BadOrb** gameObject

Line 25: `Destroy(gameObject);`

- ◆ **EnergyPulse** hit something, so it is destroyed and disappears

Line 28: `Destroy(gameObject);`

- ◆ When **EnergyPulse** hits something it is destroyed and disappears
- ◆ This is executed when **EnergyPulse** hits anything other than a `BadOrb` GameObject

Have a go hero – analyzing the code for the second level of play

Scene2 is very similar to **Scene1**. It's included to show the ability to have a game with more than one level of play. Switching to the `PlayStateScene2` State is just as easy as switching to any other State. I did not explain the code for **Scene2** because it would be redundant analysis. You already know all the fundamentals and concepts to be able to look at the code and know how it works. The challenge for you is to analyze the classes and code for **Scene2**, and in the process realize that you now have the ability to do just that, read and understand code.

Pop quiz – knowing which Unity methods to call

Q1. Using code, what are the two ways to move a GameObject in a game?

Q2. When applying a force to a GameObject to move it, what method should be used? (Hint: it's not `Update()`).

Q3. When wanting to fire a projectile that doesn't even exist in the scene, how do you get one to appear in the game?

Q4. To display buttons and text on the game screen, what Unity method is used?

Summary

Even though this simple game wasn't much to look at, its sole purpose was to show you how small sections of code are brought together to form a game. We used C# to turn Rigidbody physics on and off for **Player**, and moved the Player using physics forces. A couple of extra cameras were added to provide two ways to follow the Player. We created a scoring system that's displayed on screen during the game. Finally, we covered detecting and using collision and trigger events.

In the final chapter, we'll review your new C# skills and where to go from here to continue your education.

11

Summarizing Your New Coding Skills

When you initially started with this book, all the little details about programming looked like a treacherous mountain to climb. Every step up the mountain was perceived as the one that would just be too difficult to take. Learning to write C# code looked nearly impossible to learn. Not because each step is difficult, but because it looked like a mountain of information to overcome. Then the journey began and a funny thing happened along the way. Each step became just another step. Before long, the top was reached and the goal was accomplished. All that initial fear and worry was nothing more than overzealous imagination.

Now that the top is reached, we'll turn around and look at the new skills you just learned, and mention some things that weren't learned during your hike up this mountain.

In this chapter we will cover the following topics:

◆ Review the goal of this book

◆ Look at the C# you learned, and didn't learn

◆ Look at the State Machine as a design choice

◆ Talk about furthering your education

Let's see where to go from here.

Coding a Unity Project

Unity projects are usually about the game being created, and not the code used to control the game. The State Machine was the project for this book; not the actual game. The simple game was just a collection of examples to demonstrate coding to access some of Unity's features.

The point of this book is to teach the basics of programming using C#. The State Machine allowed me to teach you about C# classes that were not Unity scripts. As you learned, not all classes have to be a script attached to a GameObject. If a class doesn't use any of Unity's magic methods, such as `Update()` and `Start()`, and none of the variables need to appear in the **Inspector** panel, then you could just create a regular C# class instead of a Component script.

None of the State classes are Components so they don't have to inherit from `MonoBehaviour`, yet they allow fine control of the game while organizing the code. Instead of having many large scripts with many `if-else` statements to determine game flow, a few compact States were used when needed.

Working with objects

We saw that in Unity, everything is an object that contains data in variables, and methods to work with the data. For instance, the `Player` object knew its color, how fast it could move, and that it could shoot projectiles. The projectile object knew how long it would exist, how fast it travelled, and what to do when it encountered another object. The objects know what to do because their behaviors were defined in a class file.

This interaction between objects is possible because they could talk to each other by using dot syntax communication. The class defines what an object should or shouldn't do when encountering with another object. The `Player` object knew it should try to hover over other GameObjects. However, if it instead collided with certain GameObjects, `Player` and the other GameObjects communicated with each other to cause specific actions to take place, such as changing the score.

Even though classes are nice from a coding point of view, the basic thing to understand is that a class simply consists of the two main building blocks of programming, variables and methods.

No matter what feature C# may have that makes writing code easier, everything revolves around variables to store data, and methods to act on the data. That's why the first goal of this book was to help you understand these building blocks.

Scratching the surface of C# programming

We learned many ways to work with data. The code inside a method is where all the work is performed on the data, such as using the data to make decisions or modifying the data value. Even when Dot Syntax extracted data from another objects, all the work was performed in a method.

The C# code we used was rather basic, but we accomplished everything needed to create our game. Once again, that was the purpose of this book, to teach you the fundamental concepts of programming and use basic C# coding techniques to get the job done.

There are more C# techniques we could have used to make our code more efficient, and you may want to learn more about C#. But if you just want to understand enough C# to get some scripts written that are basic and easy to understand, then that's fine.

Understanding concepts can take a while to sink in before the lights turn on. So keeping the learning list short is important for a beginning programmer. This allows the basic concepts to be well-established before trying to learn some of the more advanced features of C# programming.

Looking at even more C# features

Some of the C# areas we didn't cover that you may want to look into are enumerations and switch statements. This could be useful to use to replace a lot of `if-else` statements when making logic decisions.

C# properties are slightly more advanced version of using variables. They allow more control over accessing or setting the data the variable will store.

Then there's even more advanced features such as the use of delegates or reflection features, which are definitely not appropriate for a beginner's book.

It all depends on what your goal happens to be, to get some simple scripts written or to make your code as efficient as possible with as few lines of code possible.

Just keep this simple rule in mind, *write your code simple enough so another programmer can easily understand what it does, because in six months, you'll be that other programmer.*

As you write your scripts, you know how it works and what it's supposed to do because you're writing it right now. In six months, all you will have is a vague memory of the code you write today, if you're lucky. I will bet that if your code isn't easily understandable, then in six month or more when you need to make a change, you'll come back and look at your code and say "What the heck is this trying to do? Who wrote this mess?"

Looking at even more Unity features

There are many Unity specific items not covered in this C# book. For example, we didn't specifically cover saving any data to disk, nor did we look at how to use coroutines.

This book would have been extremely long if everything about scripting was covered. It would have been much larger than the **Scripting Reference**. It also would have made you think you needed to learn everything before diving in and trying to write a code.

Remember that the Unity documentation is there so you don't have to know everything. With the basics of writing code under your belt, you can look into the **Reference Manual** and **Scripting Reference** to get and understand the code you want when it's needed.

The **Scripting Reference** documents all the behaviors you can apply to a GameObject. When you look in the **Scripting Reference** for a specific behavior, you are given the methods and variables needed, and some code to show you how to use them. Sometimes you may be able to use the example code as it is; but sometimes you'll need to modify the example code to fit your needs.

The point is, you know the fundamentals of variables, methods, and Dot Syntax. It will now be a lot easier to look at code examples in the **Scripting Reference** and figure out the details of its operation, and then apply it according to your needs.

Controlling the game with a State Machine

Just like your daily routines, you follow certain patterns that are comfortable to you. Why is that? Probably because it's easy for you and they're etched in your brain; they're habits.

Whatever it is you do; sort your laundry, build a sandwich, wash the dishes, work with Unity, you will eventually develop a routine pattern that you'll follow and like. You can equally believe that you will establish a pattern for writing scripts, too. Right now, after reading this book, you may already have some idea of how you will write and add scripts to GameObjects. Maybe you're already quite proficient at everything in Unity except for the scripting part. All you may want is to write some scripts and attach them to your GameObjects, then get back to doing the fun stuff.

How you design your scripts to control your game can be simple and neat, or if you're not careful, it could turn into a spaghetti nightmare that will make you pull out your hair. Just haphazardly writing scripts will not make you happy, especially if you need to make changes in your game flow at a later time.

Using a State Machine is a design pattern choice

As you discovered, each active State allows you to control what Unity does and what it displays.

It organized our code making it simple, neat, and easy to follow. I happen to like it. You may have decided that you don't like the idea of a State Machine after seeing the version in this book. Every programmer develops their own routine for coding. The point is, you will decide what's easiest for you and establish a pattern that's comfortable.

Besides showing you why I like State Machines, I also exposed you to writing regular C# classes. I also expanded a little into using a C# interface as well. A C# interface could be used easily with Unity Component classes as well. I just happened to need this C# feature for the State Machine classes.

Using the State Machine at the GameObject level

Our State Machine was used to control the whole game. You could just as easily use this State Machine design pattern at the GameObject level as well.

Our game State Machine used the `StateManager` object. This was a Component attached to the empty **GameManager** in the **Scenes** panel. Its primary job was to know which State was active during the game.

For a visible GameObject such as an enemy, you could control its allowed actions for various conditions. You would basically name the attached Component script something like `EnemyStateManager`. The following graphic shows a possible enemy State Machine:

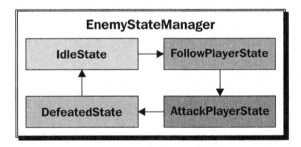

An alternate to using this type of State Machine is that you could code a GameObject State Machine using a combination of a C# enumeration and a switch statement.

That's the neat thing about programming. There are countless way to write code to get the desired result and behavior.

I personally prefer to have many very small class files that do one task rather than having one huge class file that does many things by using endless lines of `if-else` statements or long switch statements. You will eventually determine your preferred way of doing things.

Pulling all the little C# pieces together

It's one thing to study a bunch of tutorials about C# to learn the programming jargon and syntax. That's actually the easy part. The tough part for beginners is to understand how to bring it all together into a project.

I personally like using the State Machine because it doubles as an outline or mind map for a Unity project. Then it's just a matter of creating the class files corresponding to the mind map, and coding the behavior that each class will perform.

This is especially helpful for the beginner programmer. You've learned many things about C# in specific little chunks, such as variables, methods, `if` statements, `for` loops, and lists. Trying to combine all these little chunks of new knowledge to create a game can seem like a mountain has to be climbed. Separating code into many little class files makes each class easier to deal with, as opposed to having a class file that has long pages and does everything.

The only way to get good at programming is to actually write code. The usual advice to beginner programmers is to practice, practice, and practice by doing small projects. That advice is good, but let's be realistic. You probably already have a Unity project started that just needs some scripts written. Do you really feel like going off on some tangent to create some little learning projects that don't interest you? Will you really be able to concentrate on learning as you practice coding when all you can think about is your game project?

By separating your code into smaller, dedicated classes, you essentially have your little project to practice on. Plus you'll feel so much better having completed something you actually needed.

Learning more after this book

From now on, you should have a much easier time reading and watching tutorials because you won't be wondering what things such as `public`, `private`, `float`, and `void` mean. You'll now know what to concentrate on when seeing the code written by others instead of being confused by mundane things such as access modifiers, data types, and method return types.

Visit my favorite website for C#

I actually only have one website that I really like for learning C# specific code:

   ◆   C# Tutorial: Dot Net Perls: You can find this at `http://www.dotnetperls.com`.

Other than this one website, just do an Internet search for C# and you will get countless websites devoted to C# coding.

Visit my favorite websites for Unity coding:

Let me say that the tutorials on Unity's website have improved greatly. If I am looking for some really specific coding content, my first stop is :

Unity Answers: You can find this at `http://answers.unity3d.com/index.html`.

I also have a few websites that I browse for examples to create Unity scripts and they are as follows:

   ◆   *BurgZerg Arcade*: You can find this tutorial at
       `http://www.burgzergarcade.com/tutorials`

   ◆   *Unity Gems*: You can find this tutorial at `http://unitygems.com`

   ◆   *Tornado Twins*: You can find this tutorial at `http://www.youtube.com/user/TornadoTwins`

Another website that I use is a pay website, but it also provides free content:

Unity Cookie: You can find this tutorial at `http://cgcookie.com/unity/`

The Packt Publishing website has a multitude of books on Unity. You can find Unity books by Packt at `http://www.packtpub.com/books?keys=unity`.

Summary

In this final chapter, we reviewed the goals of this book to teach you the C# fundamentals. C# allows the flexibility to write and use regular class files as well as Unity script files. Also, we covered why I believe using a State Machine helps to organize a project.

Hopefully, this book will have helped you to totally understand the basics of C#. If so, you now have the ability to further your C# studies and you'll find it easier to understand the tutorials available on the Internet.

I hope I was able to help you overcome the perceived mountain of fear you may have had before reading this book. Remember, code is just a series of simple steps, so take one step at a time, just like climbing that mountain.

A
Initial State Machine files

These are the State Machine files mentioned at the beginning of *Chapter 9, Start Building a Game and Get the Basic Structure Running*, necessary for our Unity project.

- BeginState
- SetupState
- PlayStateScene1_1: (1 of 2 available States in Scene1)
- PlayStateScene1_2: (2 of 2 available States in Scene1)
- WonStateScene1
- LostStateScene1
- PlayStateScene2
- WonStateScene2
- LostStateScene2
- StateManager
- IStateBase

This is how the files should be coded to begin *Chapter 9, Start Building a Game and Get the Basic Structure Running.* These make the State Machine functional for switching States and Scenes.

Each one will be modified as we progress through *Chapters 9, Start Building a Game and Get the Basic Structure Running* and *Chapter 10, Moving Around, Collisions, and Keeping Score*.

BeginState

```
using UnityEngine;
using Assets.Code.Interfaces;

namespace Assets.Code.States
{
  public class BeginState : IStateBase
  {
    private StateManager manager;

    public BeginState (StateManager managerRef)
    {
      manager = managerRef;
      if(Application.loadedLevelName != "Scene0")
        Application.LoadLevel("Scene0");
    }

    public void StateUpdate ()
    {
      if (Input.GetKeyUp (KeyCode.Space))
      {
        manager.SwitchState (new SetupState (manager));
      }
    }

    public void ShowIt ()
    {
      Debug.Log ("In BeginState");
    }
  }
}
```

SetupState

```
using UnityEngine;
using Assets.Code.Interfaces;
using System.Collections;

namespace Assets.Code.States
{
  public class SetupState : IStateBase
  {
```

```
      private StateManager manager;

      public SetupState (StateManager managerRef)
      {
        manager = managerRef;
        if(Application.loadedLevelName != "Scene0")
          Application.LoadLevel("Scene0");
      }

      public void StateUpdate ()
      {
        if (Input.GetKeyUp (KeyCode.Space))
        {
          manager.SwitchState (new
            PlayStateScene1_1 (manager));
        }
      }

      public void ShowIt ()
      {
        Debug.Log ("In SetupState");
      }
    }
}
```

PlayStateScene1_1: (1 of 2 available States in Scene1)

```
using UnityEngine;
using Assets.Code.Interfaces;

namespace Assets.Code.States
{
  public class PlayStateScene1_1 : IStateBase
  {
    private StateManager manager;

    public PlayStateScene1_1 (StateManager managerRef)
    {
      manager = managerRef;
      if(Application.loadedLevelName != "Scene1")
        Application.LoadLevel("Scene1");
    }
```

```
    public void StateUpdate()
    {
      if (Input.GetKeyUp (KeyCode.Space))
      {
      manager.SwitchState (new
        WonStateScene1 (manager));
      }

      if (Input.GetKeyUp (KeyCode.Return))
      {
        manager.SwitchState (new
          LostStateScene1 (manager));
      }
    }

    public void ShowIt()
    {
      Debug.Log("In PlayStateScene1_1");
    }
  }
}
```

PlayStateScene1_2: (2 of 2 available States in Scene1)

```
using UnityEngine;
using Assets.Code.Interfaces;

namespace Assets.Code.States
{
  public class PlayStateScene1_2 : IStateBase
  {
    private StateManager manager;

    public PlayStateScene1_2 (StateManager managerRef)
    {
      manager = managerRef;
      if(Application.loadedLevelName != "Scene1")
        Application.LoadLevel("Scene1");
    }

    public void StateUpdate()
    {
      if (Input.GetKeyUp (KeyCode.Space))
```

```
        {
          manager.SwitchState (new
            WonStateScene1 (manager));
        }

        if (Input.GetKeyUp (KeyCode.Return))
        {
          manager.SwitchState (new
            LostStateScene1 (manager));
        }
      }

    public void ShowIt ()
    {
      Debug.Log("In PlayStateScene1_2");
    }
  }
}
```

WonStateScene1

```
using UnityEngine;
using Assets.Code.Interfaces;

namespace Assets.Code.States
{
  public class WonStateScene1 : IStateBase
  {
    private StateManager manager;

    public WonStateScene1 (StateManager managerRef)
    {
      manager = managerRef;
      if(Application.loadedLevelName != "Scene0")
        Application.LoadLevel("Scene0");
    }

    public void StateUpdate ()
    {
      if (Input.GetKeyUp (KeyCode.Space))
      {
        manager.SwitchState (new
          PlayStateScene2 (manager));
```

```
        }
    }

    public void ShowIt()
    {
        Debug.Log("In WonStateScene1");
    }
    }
}
```

LostStateScene1

```
using UnityEngine;
using Assets.Code.Interfaces;

namespace Assets.Code.States
{
    public class LostStateScene1 : IStateBase
    {
        private StateManager manager;

        public LostStateScene1 (StateManager managerRef)
        {
            manager = managerRef;
            if(Application.loadedLevelName != "Scene0")
                Application.LoadLevel("Scene0");
        }

        public void StateUpdate()
        {
            if (Input.GetKeyUp (KeyCode.Space))
            {
                manager.SwitchState (new
                    PlayStateScene1_1 (manager));
            }

            if (Input.GetKeyUp (KeyCode.Return))
            {
                manager.Restart();
            }
        }

        public void ShowIt()
```

```
    {
      Debug.Log("In LostStateScene1");
    }
  }
}
```

PlayStateScene2

```
using UnityEngine;
using Assets.Code.Interfaces;

namespace Assets.Code.States
{
  public class PlayStateScene2 : IStateBase
  {
    private StateManager manager;

    public PlayStateScene2 (StateManager managerRef)
    {
      manager = managerRef;
      if(Application.loadedLevelName != "Scene2")
        Application.LoadLevel("Scene2");
    }

    public void StateUpdate()
    {
      if (Input.GetKeyUp (KeyCode.Space))
      {
        manager.SwitchState (new
          WonStateScene2 (manager));
      }

      if (Input.GetKeyUp (KeyCode.Return))
      {
        manager.SwitchState (new
          LostStateScene2 (manager));
      }
    }

    public void ShowIt()
    {
      Debug.Log("In PlayStateScene2");
    }
  }
}
```

WonStateScene2

```
using UnityEngine;
using Assets.Code.Interfaces;

namespace Assets.Code.States
{
  public class WonStateScene2 : IStateBase
  {
    private StateManager manager;

    public WonStateScene2 (StateManager managerRef)
    {
      manager = managerRef;
      if(Application.loadedLevelName != "Scene0")
        Application.LoadLevel("Scene0");
    }

    public void StateUpdate()
    {
      if (Input.GetKeyUp (KeyCode.Space))
      {
        manager.Restart();
      }
    }

    public void ShowIt()
    {
      Debug.Log("In WonStateScene2");
    }
  }
}
```

LostStateScene2

```
using UnityEngine;
using Assets.Code.Interfaces;

namespace Assets.Code.States
{
  public class LostStateScene2 : IStateBase
  {
    private StateManager manager;
```

```
    public LostStateScene2 (StateManager managerRef)
    {
      manager = managerRef;
      if(Application.loadedLevelName != "Scene0")
        Application.LoadLevel("Scene0");
    }

    public void StateUpdate()
    {
      if (Input.GetKeyUp (KeyCode.Space))
      {
        manager.SwitchState (new
          PlayStateScene2 (manager));
      }

      if (Input.GetKeyUp (KeyCode.Return))
      {
        manager.Restart();
      }
    }

    public void ShowIt()
    {
      Debug.Log("In LostStateScene2");
    }
  }
}
```

StateManager

```
using UnityEngine;
using Assets.Code.States;
using Assets.Code.Interfaces;

public class StateManager : MonoBehaviour
{
    private IStateBase activeState;

  private static StateManager instanceRef;

  void Awake ()
  {
    if(instanceRef == null)
```

```
      {
        instanceRef = this;
        DontDestroyOnLoad(gameObject);
      }
      else
      {
        DestroyImmediate(gameObject);
      }
    }

    void Start ()
    {
      activeState = new BeginState(this);
    }

      void Update()
      {
      if (activeState != null)
            activeState.StateUpdate();
      }

    void OnGUI()
    {
      if(activeState != null)
        activeState.ShowIt();
    }

      public void SwitchState(IStateBase newState)
      {
          activeState = newState;
      }

    public void Restart()
    {
      Destroy(gameObject);
      Application.LoadLevel("Scene0");
    }
  }
```

IStateBase

```
namespace Assets.Code.Interfaces
{
  public interface IStateBase
  {
    void StateUpdate();
    void ShowIt();
  }
}
```

B

Completed code files for Chapters 9 and 10

BeginState

```
using UnityEngine;
using Assets.Code.Interfaces;

namespace Assets.Code.States
{
  public class BeginState : IStateBase
  {
    private StateManager manager;

    public BeginState (StateManager managerRef)
    {
      manager = managerRef;
      if(Application.loadedLevelName != "Scene0")
        Application.LoadLevel("Scene0");
    }

    public void StateUpdate ()
    {
    }

    public void ShowIt ()
    {
      GUI.DrawTexture(new Rect(0, 0, Screen.width,
            Screen.height),
        manager.gameDataRef.beginStateSplash,
```

```
            ScaleMode.StretchToFill);

        if (GUI.Button(new Rect(10, 10, 250, 60),
            "Press Here or Any Key to Continue") ||
            Input.anyKeyDown)
        {
            manager.SwitchState (new SetupState (manager));
        }
    }
  }
}
```

SetupState

```
using UnityEngine;
using Assets.Code.Interfaces;
using System.Collections;

namespace Assets.Code.States
{
  public class SetupState : IStateBase
  {
    private StateManager manager;
    private GameObject player;
    private PlayerControl controller;

    public SetupState (StateManager managerRef)
    {
      manager = managerRef;
      if(Application.loadedLevelName != "Scene0")
        Application.LoadLevel("Scene0");

      player = GameObject.Find("Player");
      controller = player.GetComponent<PlayerControl>();
    }

    public void StateUpdate ()
    {
      if(!Input.GetButton("Jump"))
        controller.transform.Rotate(0,
        controller.setupSpinSpeed * Time.deltaTime, 0);
    }
```

```
public void StateFixedUpdate()
{
}

public void ShowIt ()
{
  GUI.Box(new Rect(Screen.width - 110,10,100,25),
    string.Format("Lives left: "+
    manager.gameDataRef.playerLives));

  GUI.Box(new Rect(Screen.width -110,40,100,120),
    "Player Lives");

  if(GUI.Button(new Rect(Screen.width - 100,70,80,20),
    "5"))
    manager.gameDataRef.SetPlayerLives(5);

  if(GUI.Button(new Rect(Screen.width - 100,100,80,20),
    "10"))  manager.gameDataRef.SetPlayerLives(10);

  if(GUI.Button(new Rect(Screen.width - 100,130,80,20),
    "Can't Lose"))
              manager.gameDataRef.SetPlayerLives(1000);

  GUI.Box(new Rect(10,10,100,180), "Player Color");

  if(GUI.Button(new Rect(20,40,80,20), "Red"))
    controller.PickedColor(controller.red);

  if(GUI.Button(new Rect(20,70,80,20), "Blue"))
    controller.PickedColor(controller.blue);

  if(GUI.Button(new Rect(20,100,80,20), "Green"))
    controller.PickedColor(controller.green);

 if(GUI.Button(new Rect(20,130,80,20), "Yellow"))
    controller.PickedColor(controller.yellow);

  if(GUI.Button(new Rect(20,160,80,20), "White"))
    controller.PickedColor(controller.white);

  GUI.Label(new Rect(Screen.width/2 -95,
    Screen.height - 100, 190, 30),
    "Hold Spacebar to pause rotation");
```

```
        if (GUI.Button(new Rect(Screen.width/2 -100,
          Screen.height - 50, 200, 40),
          "Click Here or Press 'P' to Play ") ||
          Input.GetKeyUp(KeyCode.P))
        {
          manager.SwitchState (new PlayStateScene1_1
            (manager));
          player.transform.position =
            new Vector3(50, .5f, 40);
        }
      }
    }
  }
```

PlayStateScene1_1: (1 of 2 available States in Scene1)

```
using UnityEngine;
using System.Collections;
using Assets.Code.Interfaces;

namespace Assets.Code.States
{
  public class PlayStateScene1_1 : IStateBase
  {
    private StateManager manager;
    private GameObject player;

    public PlayStateScene1_1 (StateManager managerRef)
    {
      manager = managerRef;
      if(Application.loadedLevelName != "Scene1")
        Application.LoadLevel("Scene1");

      player = GameObject.Find("Player");
      player.rigidbody.isKinematic = false;

      foreach(GameObject camera in                 manager.
gameDataRef.cameras)
      {
        if(camera.name != "LookAt Camera")
          camera.SetActive(false);
        else
          camera.SetActive(true);
      }
    }
```

```
    public void StateUpdate()
    {
      if(manager.gameDataRef.playerLives <= 0)
      {
        manager.SwitchState(new
LostStateScene1(manager));
        manager.gameDataRef.ResetPlayer();
        player.rigidbody.isKinematic = true;
        player.transform.position = new
          Vector3(50, .5f, 40);
      }

      if(manager.gameDataRef.score >= 2)
      {
        manager.SwitchState(new
WonStateScene1(manager));
        player.rigidbody.isKinematic = true;
        player.transform.position = new
          Vector3(50, .5f, 40);
      }
    }

    public void ShowIt()
    {
      GUI.Box(new Rect(10,10,100,25),
        string.Format("Score: "+              manager.gameDataRef.
score));

      if(GUI.Button(new
        Rect(Screen.width/2 - 130, 10, 260, 30),
        string.Format("Click here or Press 2 for
        Level 1, State 2"))
        || Input.GetKeyUp(KeyCode.Alpha2))
      {
        manager.SwitchState(new
PlayStateScene1_2(manager));
      }

      GUI.Box(new Rect(Screen.width - 110,10,100,25),
        string.Format("Lives left: "+              manager.
gameDataRef.playerLives));
    }
  }
}
```

PlayStateScene1_2: (2 of 2 available States in Scene1)

```
using UnityEngine;
using Assets.Code.Interfaces;

namespace Assets.Code.States
{
  public class PlayStateScene1_2 : IStateBase
  {
    private StateManager manager;
    private GameObject player;
    private PlayerControl controller;

    public PlayStateScene1_2 (StateManager managerRef)
    {
      manager = managerRef;
      player = GameObject.Find("Player");
      controller = player.GetComponent<PlayerControl>();

      foreach(GameObject camera in          manager.
gameDataRef.cameras)
      {
        if(camera.name != "Following Camera")
          camera.SetActive(false);
        else
          camera.SetActive(true);
      }
    }

    public void StateUpdate()
    {
      if(manager.gameDataRef.playerLives <= 0)
      {
        manager.SwitchState(new
LostStateScene1(manager));
        manager.gameDataRef.ResetPlayer();
        player.rigidbody.isKinematic = true;
        player.transform.position = new
        Vector3(50, .5f, 40);
      }

      if(manager.gameDataRef.score >= 2)
      {
```

```
            manager.SwitchState(new
WonStateScene1(manager));
        player.rigidbody.isKinematic = true;
        player.transform.position = new
          Vector3(50, .5f, 40);
    }

    if(Input.GetKeyDown(KeyCode.LeftControl))
    {
      controller.FireEnergyPulse();
    }
  }


  public void ShowIt()
  {
    GUI.Box(new Rect(10,10,100,25),
      string.Format("Score: "+                    manager.gameDataRef.
score));

    if(GUI.Button(new
      Rect(Screen.width/2 - 130, 10, 260, 30),
      string.Format("Click here or Press 1 for
      Level 1, State 1"))
      || Input.GetKeyUp(KeyCode.Alpha1))
    {
      manager.SwitchState(new
PlayStateScene1_1(manager));
    }

    GUI.Box(new Rect(Screen.width - 110,10,100,25),
      string.Format("Lives left: "+                manager.
gameDataRef.playerLives));
  }
 }
}
```

WonStateScene1

```
using UnityEngine;
using Assets.Code.Interfaces;

namespace Assets.Code.States
{
  public class WonStateScene1 : IStateBase
```

```
    {
      private StateManager manager;

      public WonStateScene1 (StateManager managerRef)
      {
        manager = managerRef;
        if(Application.loadedLevelName != "Scene0")
          Application.LoadLevel("Scene0");

        manager.gameDataRef.SetScore();
      }

      public void StateUpdate()
      {
      }

      public void ShowIt()
      {
        GUI.DrawTexture(new
          Rect(0, 0, Screen.width, Screen.height),
          manager.gameDataRef.wonStateSplash,
          ScaleMode.StretchToFill);

        if (GUI.Button(new Rect(10, 10, 250, 30),
          "Click Here or Space key for next Level") ||
          Input.GetKeyUp (KeyCode.Space))
        {
          manager.SwitchState (new
          PlayStateScene2 (manager));
        }
      }
    }
  }
}
```

LostStateScene1

```
using UnityEngine;
using Assets.Code.Interfaces;

namespace Assets.Code.States
{
  public class LostStateScene1 : IStateBase
  {
```

```
    private StateManager manager;

    public LostStateScene1 (StateManager managerRef)
    {
      manager = managerRef;
      if(Application.loadedLevelName != "Scene0")
        Application.LoadLevel("Scene0");
    }

    public void StateUpdate()
    {
    }

    public void ShowIt()
    {
      GUI.DrawTexture(new
        Rect(0, 0, Screen.width, Screen.height),
        manager.gameDataRef.lostStateSplash,
        ScaleMode.StretchToFill);

      if (GUI.Button(new Rect(10, 10, 270, 30),
        "Click Here or Space key to repeat Level") ||
        Input.GetKeyUp (KeyCode.Space))
      {
        manager.SwitchState (new
        PlayStateScene1_1 (manager));
      }

      if (GUI.Button(new Rect(10, 50, 270, 30),
        "Click Here or Return key to Restart Game") ||
        Input.GetKeyUp (KeyCode.Return))
      {
        manager.Restart();
      }
    }
  }
}
```

PlayStateScene2

```
using UnityEngine;
using Assets.Code.Interfaces;

namespace Assets.Code.States
```

```
{
  public class PlayStateScene2 : IStateBase
  {
    private StateManager manager;
    private GameObject player;
    private PlayerControl controller;

    public PlayStateScene2 (StateManager managerRef)
    {
      manager = managerRef;
      if(Application.loadedLevelName != "Scene2")
        Application.LoadLevel("Scene2");

      player = GameObject.Find("Player");
      controller = player.GetComponent<PlayerControl>();
      player.rigidbody.isKinematic = false;

      foreach(var camera in manager.gameDataRef.cameras)
      {
        if(camera.name != "Following Camera")
          camera.SetActive(false);
        else
          camera.SetActive(true);
      }
    }

    public void StateUpdate()
    {
      if(manager.gameDataRef.playerLives <= 0)
      {
        manager.SwitchState(new
LostStateScene2(manager));
        manager.gameDataRef.ResetPlayer();
        player.rigidbody.isKinematic = true;
        player.transform.position = new
          Vector3(50, .5f, 40);
      }

      if(manager.gameDataRef.score >= 5)
      {
        manager.SwitchState(new
WonStateScene2(manager));
        player.rigidbody.isKinematic = true;
      }
```

```
    if(Input.GetKey(KeyCode.LeftControl))
    {
      controller.FireEnergyPulse();
    }
  }

  public void ShowIt()
  {
    GUI.Box(new Rect(10,10,100,25),
      string.Format("Score: "+                 manager.gameDataRef.
score));

    GUI.Box(new Rect(Screen.width - 110,10,100,25),
      string.Format("Lives left: "+              manager.
gameDataRef.playerLives));
  }
 }
}
```

WonStateScene2

```
using UnityEngine;
using Assets.Code.Interfaces;

namespace Assets.Code.States
{
  public class WonStateScene2 : IStateBase
  {
    private StateManager manager;

    public WonStateScene2 (StateManager managerRef)
    {
      manager = managerRef;
      if(Application.loadedLevelName != "Scene0")
        Application.LoadLevel("Scene0");
    }

    public void StateUpdate()
    {
    }

    public void ShowIt()
    {
      GUI.DrawTexture(new
```

```
            Rect(0, 0, Screen.width, Screen.height),
            manager.gameDataRef.wonStateSplash,
            ScaleMode.StretchToFill);

        if (GUI.Button(new Rect(10, 10, 270, 30),
          "Click Here or Return key to Restart Game") ||
          Input.GetKeyUp (KeyCode.Return))
        {
          manager.Restart();
        }
      }
    }
  }
```

LostStateScene2

```
using UnityEngine;
using Assets.Code.Interfaces;

namespace Assets.Code.States
{
  public class LostStateScene2 : IStateBase
  {
    private StateManager manager;

    public LostStateScene2 (StateManager managerRef)
    {
      manager = managerRef;
      if(Application.loadedLevelName != "Scene0")
        Application.LoadLevel("Scene0");
    }

    public void StateUpdate()
    {
    }

    public void ShowIt()
    {
      GUI.DrawTexture(new
        Rect(0, 0, Screen.width, Screen.height),
        manager.gameDataRef.lostStateSplash,
        ScaleMode.StretchToFill);
```

```
    if (GUI.Button(new Rect(10, 10, 270, 30),
      "Click Here or Space key to repeat Level") ||
      Input.GetKeyUp (KeyCode.Space))
    {
      manager.SwitchState (new
        PlayStateScene2 (manager));
    }

    if (GUI.Button(new Rect(10, 50, 270, 30),
      "Click Here or Return key to Restart Game") ||
      Input.GetKeyUp (KeyCode.Return))
    {
      manager.Restart ();
    }
    }
  }
}
```

StateManager

```
using UnityEngine;
using Assets.Code.States;
using Assets.Code.Interfaces;

public class StateManager : MonoBehaviour
{
  private IStateBase activeState;

  [HideInInspector]
  public GameData gameDataRef;

  private static StateManager instanceRef;

  void Awake ()
  {
    if(instanceRef == null)
    {
      instanceRef = this;
      DontDestroyOnLoad(gameObject);
    }
    else
    {
      DestroyImmediate(gameObject);
```

```
        }
    }

    void Start ()
    {
        activeState = new BeginState(this);
        gameDataRef = GetComponent<GameData>();
    }

        void Update()
        {
        if (activeState != null)
                activeState.StateUpdate();
        }

    void OnGUI()
    {
        if(activeState != null)
            activeState.ShowIt();
    }

        public void SwitchState(IStateBase newState)
        {
            activeState = newState;
        }

    public void Restart()
    {
        Destroy(gameObject);
        Application.LoadLevel("Scene0");
    }
}
```

PlayerControl

```
using UnityEngine;
using System.Collections;

public class PlayerControl : MonoBehaviour
{
    public float setupSpinSpeed = 50.0f;
    public float speed = 16.0f;
    public float rotationSpeed = 0.60f;
```

```csharp
    public float hoverPower = 3.5f;
    public Rigidbody projectile;

    public Color red = Color.red;
    public Color blue = Color.blue;
    public Color green = Color.green;
    public Color yellow = Color.yellow;
    public Color white = Color.white;

    private GameData gameDataRef;

    void Start ()
    {
        gameDataRef =                        GameObject.Find("GameManager").
GetComponent<GameData>();
    }

    void FixedUpdate()
    {
        float foreAndAft = Input.GetAxis ("Vertical") * speed;
        float rotation =
            Input.GetAxis ("Horizontal") * rotationSpeed;
        rigidbody.AddRelativeForce (0, 0, foreAndAft);
        rigidbody.AddTorque (0, rotation, 0);
    }

    void OnTriggerStay(Collider other)
    {
        rigidbody.AddForce(Vector3.up * hoverPower);
    }

    void OnTriggerEnter(Collider other)
    {
        if(other.gameObject.tag == "GoodOrb")
        {
            gameDataRef.score += 1;
            Destroy(other.gameObject);
        }
    }

    void OnCollisionEnter(Collision collidedWith)
    {
        if(collidedWith.gameObject.tag == "BadOrb")
        {
```

```csharp
            gameDataRef.playerLives -= 1;
            Destroy(collidedWith.gameObject);
        }
    }

    public void FireEnergyPulse()
    {
        Rigidbody clone;
        clone = Instantiate(projectile, transform.position,
transform.rotation) as Rigidbody;
        clone.transform.Translate(0, .5f, 2.1f);
        clone.velocity =                    transform.
TransformDirection(Vector3.forward * 50);
    }

    public void PickedColor (Color playerColor)
    {
        renderer.material.color = playerColor;
    }
}
```

GameData

```csharp
using UnityEngine;
using System.Collections.Generic;

public class GameData : MonoBehaviour
{
    public Texture2D beginStateSplash;
    public Texture2D lostStateSplash;
    public Texture2D wonStateSplash;

    public List<GameObject> cameras;

    private int playerLivesSelected = 2;
    private int sceneBeginningScore;

    [HideInInspector]
    public int playerLives;
    [HideInInspector]
    public int score;

    void Start ()
```

```
  {
    playerLives = playerLivesSelected;
  }

  public void ResetPlayer()
  {
    playerLives = playerLivesSelected;
    score = sceneBeginningScore;
  }

  public void SetPlayerLives(int livesSelected)
  {
    playerLivesSelected = livesSelected;
    playerLives = livesSelected;
  }

  public void SetScore()
  {
    sceneBeginningScore = score;
  }
}
```

LookAtPlayer

```
using UnityEngine;
using System.Collections;

public class LookAtPlayer : MonoBehaviour
{
  private Transform playerPosition;

  void Start()
  {
    playerPosition = GameObject.Find("Player").transform;
  }

  void LateUpdate( )
  {
    transform.LookAt(playerPosition);
  }
}
```

FollowingPlayer

```
using UnityEngine;
using System.Collections;

public class FollowingPlayer : MonoBehaviour
{
  public float cameraHeight = 17.0f;
  public float cameraDistance = 17.0f;

  private Transform playerPosition;

  void Start()
  {
    playerPosition = GameObject.Find("Player").transform;
  }

  void LateUpdate( )
  {
    transform.position = playerPosition.position +
      new Vector3(cameraDistance, cameraHeight,
-cameraDistance);
    transform.LookAt(playerPosition);
  }
}
```

EnergyPulsePower

```
using UnityEngine;
using System.Collections;

public class EnergyPulsePower : MonoBehaviour
{
  public float pulseDuration = 1f;

  public Transform goodOrb;

  void Update()
  {
    pulseDuration -= Time.deltaTime;

    if(pulseDuration <= 0)
```

```
        Destroy(gameObject);
    }

    void OnTriggerEnter(Collider other)
    {
      if(other.gameObject.tag == "BadOrb")
      {
        Instantiate(goodOrb, other.transform.position,          other.
transform.rotation);
        GameObject.Find("GameManager).
          GetComponent<GameDate>().playerLives += 1;
        Destroy(other.gameObject);
        Destroy(gameObject);
      }
      else
        Destroy(gameObject);
    }
}
```

IStateBase

```
namespace Assets.Code.Interfaces
{
  public interface IStateBase
  {
    void StateUpdate();
    void ShowIt();
  }
}
```

C
Pop Quiz Answers

Chapter 1, Discovering Your Hidden Scripting Skills

Pop quiz – dealing with scripts

Q1	The false perception that writing code is too difficult.
Q2	Unity's Reference Manual.
Q3	None. It's a reference document, which means you look things up as you need them.
Q4	When the new file appears in Unity's Project tab, it appears with the filename in edit mode. Renaming the file immediately will make the class name the same as the filename.

Chapter 2, Introducing the Building Blocks for Unity Scripts

Pop quiz – knowing C# building blocks

Q1	To store some data that will be substituted into a script somewhere.
Q2	To execute some code that will be needed several times.
Q3	By attaching the script file to a GameObject.
Q4	To have access to variables and methods on other Components.

Chapter 3, Getting into the Details of Variables

Pop quiz – knowing how to declare a variable

Q1	Begin the name with a lowercase letter. For multiword names, a variable can only be one actual word, so spaces are removed between the words, and then capitalize the first letter of each word.
Q2	Declare the variable as public.
Q3	No, only member variables can be public.
Q4	A variable can only store one type of data, which has to be specified when it's declared.

Chapter 4, Getting into the Details of Methods

Pop quiz – understanding method operation

Q1	Specifying the type of data returned from the method, the name of the method with parenthesis, and a pair of curly braces for the code block.
Q2	To allow data to be passed into the code block.
Q3	It means the method is not returning any data to the code that called the method.
Q4	The `Update()` method is called automatically by Unity if the script inherits from `MonoBehaviour`.

Chapter 5, Making Decisions in Code

Pop quiz – understanding if statements

Q1	True or false.
Q2	The NOT operator, which is the exclamation mark (`!`).
Q3	The AND operator, which is two ampersand signs (`&&`).
Q4	The OR operator, which is a double-bat (`||`).

Pop quiz – understanding an array and a List

Q1	The location in an array, or a List, where data is stored.
Q2	The first element in an array, or a List, has an index number of zero. This is called zero indexed.
Q3	No. When an array or a List is declared, the type of data it can store is specified, and only that type can be stored in its elements.
Q4	An array cannot be dynamically expanded. Once an array is initialized, it can't change its size. This is why a List is more flexible. A List can change dynamically.

Chapter 6, Using Dot Syntax for Object Communication

Pop quiz – understanding communication between objects

Q1	It's an address for locating public variables and methods.
Q2	A reference to the object. The object itself is not stored in the variable. A reference points to the actual object so that the variables and methods of the object can be accessed.
Q3	Dot Syntax allows access to any GameObject or any of its Components, however, the variables and methods on other Components must be public.
Q4	A member variable of a Component can appear in the Inspector by making the variable public, and then a GameObject can be dragged-and-dropped into the **Property (variable)** in the **Inspector** panel.

Chapter 7, Creating the Gameplay is Just a Part of the Game

Pop quiz – using a State Machine for game control

Q1	Helps keep code very organized.
Q2	A State Machine has a controller that is a Unity script, which is attached to a GameObject. The State Machine controller in this book is named `StateManager`, which calls the methods on a particular State.
Q3	There is no limit. Use as many as needed for controlling gameflow.
Q4	A C# interface specifies the methods each State has to implement.

Chapter 8, Developing the State Machine

Pop quiz – understanding State Machine operation

Q1	The State classes also inherit the `IStateBase` interface. This means every State object is also an `IStateBase` object, allowing the `activeState` variable to store any of the State objects.
Q2	The `StateManager` script has the `Update()` method and the `OnGUI()` method. The `Update()` method calls `StateUpdate()`, and `OnGUI()` calls `ShowIt()`.
Q3	All GameObjects in the current Scene are destroyed.
Q4	Absolutely false. Adding States, removing States, and changing the order that the States can switch are a few of the greatest benefits of a State Machine.

Chapter 9, Start Building a Game and Get the Basic Structure Running

Pop quiz – understanding GameObjects

Q1	The Reference Manual and the Scripting Reference.
Q2	They are destroyed.
Q3	Each State would need to call the `GetComponent()` method which takes time. Since States already have access to `StateManager`, `StateManager` can call `GetComponent()` once and store a reference to `GameData`.
Q4	The **GameManager** GameObject does not get destroyed when the **Scene** changes. Any GameObject that is a child of **GameManager** also won't be destroyed.

Chapter 10, Moving Around, Collisions, and Keeping Score

Pop quiz – knowing which Unity methods to call

Q1	By changing the transform coordinates of the GameObject, or by adding Rigidbody to the GameObject and applying a force.
Q2	Unity highly recommends using the `FixedUpdate()` method.
Q3	First, in the **Scene** panel, a **Projectile** GameObject is created to be made into a Prefab. To get one into the running game, you have to instantiate the Prefab using the `Instantiate()` method.
Q4	The `OnGUI()` method.

Index

Thank you for buying
Learning C# by Developing Games with
Unity 3D Beginner's Guide

About Packt Publishing

Packt, pronounced 'packed', published its first book "Mastering phpMyAdmin for Effective MySQL Management" in April 2004 and subsequently continued to specialize in publishing highly focused books on specific technologies and solutions.

Our books and publications share the experiences of your fellow IT professionals in adapting and customizing today's systems, applications, and frameworks. Our solution-based books give you the knowledge and power to customize the software and technologies you're using to get the job done. Packt books are more specific and less general than the IT books you have seen in the past. Our unique business model allows us to bring you more focused information, giving you more of what you need to know, and less of what you don't.

Packt is a modern, yet unique publishing company, which focuses on producing quality, cutting-edge books for communities of developers, administrators, and newbies alike. For more information, please visit our website: www.PacktPub.com.

Writing for Packt

We welcome all inquiries from people who are interested in authoring. Book proposals should be sent to author@packtpub.com. If your book idea is still at an early stage and you would like to discuss it first before writing a formal book proposal, contact us; one of our commissioning editors will get in touch with you.

We're not just looking for published authors; if you have strong technical skills but no writing experience, our experienced editors can help you develop a writing career, or simply get some additional reward for your expertise.

C# 5 First Look

ISBN: 978-1-84968-676-1   Paperback: 138 pages

Write ultra responsive application using the new asynchronous features of C#

1. Learn about all the latest features of C#, including the asynchronous programming capabilities that promise to make apps ultra-responsive

2. Examine how C# evolved over the years to be more expressive, easier to write, and how those early design decisions enabled future innovations

3. Explore the language's bright future building applications for other platforms using the Mono Framework

XNA 4.0 Game Development by Example: Beginner's Guide – Visual Basic Edition

ISBN: 978-1-84969-240-3   Paperback: 424 pages

Create your own exciting games with Visual Basic and Microsoft XNA 4.0

1. Visual Basic edition of Kurt Jaegers' XNA 4.0 Game Development by Example. The first book to target Visual Basic developers who want to develop games with the XNA framework

2. Dive headfirst into game creation with Visual Basic and the XNA Framework

3. Four different styles of games comprising a puzzler, space shooter, multi-axis shoot 'em up, and a jump-and-run platformer

Please check **www.PacktPub.com** for information on our titles

Unity 3.x Scripting

ISBN: 978-1-84969-230-4   Paperback: 292 pages

Write efficient, reusable scripts to build custom characters, game environments, and control enemy AI in your Unity game

1. Make your characters interact with buttons and program triggered action sequences

2. Create custom characters and code dynamic objects and players' interaction with them

3. Synchronize movement of character and environmental objects

4. Add and control animations to new and existing characters

Unity 3.x Game Development Essentials

ISBN: 978-1-84969-144-4   Paperback: 488 pages

Build fully functional, professional 3D games with realistic environments, sound, dynamic effects, and more!

1. Kick start your game development, and build ready-to-play 3D games with ease.

2. Understand key concepts in game design including scripting, physics, instantiation, particle effects, and more.

3. Test & optimize your game to perfection with essential tips-and-tricks.

CPSIA information can be obtained
at www.ICGtesting.com
Printed in the USA
BVOW11s2319050218

507163BV00003B/7/P